HINTS TO VIOLIN PLAYERS.

CHAPTER I.

The Purpose of the Work.

THE extensive field over which my little works appear to have travelled has called forth a very great amount of correspondence, always eulogistic, but generally containing also many practical questions on points not fully explained in the books. On many of these points there must always be some difference of opinion, but so far as it is in my power I shall endeavour to make them clear in these pages in a manner so impartial that the reader may to a great extent rely upon his own judgment in the adoption or rejection of the hints. Many of them need not be placed before a beginner at all, inasmuch as so many minute details are apt to scare a young player. It is therefore to violin players more than beginners that I now address myself, and more especially the EARNEST STUDENT.

The Trifler.

Hundreds of violin players, so called, only trifle with the instrument—they play with the violin, not on it. They are a fraud and imposition; they are the clog of all Amateur Orchestral Societies, with their violins never perfectly in tune, and their fingers always dragging and scumbling any passage of moderate difficulty, or losing their heads, and flying off half a beat before every one else when the notes happen to be within their reach. Any one may make a mistake at times, but these triflers are always making mistakes, and smiling blandly over them, or arguing the point hotly, and plainly implying that every one else was wrong. You may tell the trifler at a glance almost by the manner in which he handles his violin—as if it were an old boot, and he were afraid of soiling his fingers with it. He never digs into severe exercises at home for a couple of hours at a time, though he may appear to be playing for that time, and generally thinks that he works tremendously hard at the instrument His very fingers and the set of his hand to the instrument will tell the sharp-eyed one that he is not a player.

The Showy Player.

A nuisance in less degree is the player who is always anxious to show off his execution for the benefit of the over-awed second violins, by making tremendous runs and skimming away into harmonics, which after all are so easy of mastery that a child can be taught in ten minutes to play a scale of them. The showy player practises a deal, but mostly at tricky music, and generally declares good music slow. He is a great man behind the scenes or at practices, but often a nobody on the platform, where he loses his head more quickly than a stupid player. He is always at his solo playing when there is an interval, or when others wish to tune, and if he plays a solo in public he comes on with a pert air and knowing smirk, which declare at once that there is no musical soul within. Great music can never come out of that poor thing. Conceit is never allied to true greatness No real artist ever puts on airs or strikes ridiculous attitudes to distract attention from the music he is rendering. These tricks are reserved for the showy player, for the small-headed musician, and for lady players, who have accentuated and exaggerated the styles of their masters. I have been able to trace the style of one great teacher thus burlesqued through several lady players, and should recognise it anywhere the moment the violin were held up. That is saddening. It reminds me of a tragedian, now forgotten, who so closely imitated Charles Kean that he spoke with the snivel, which was Kean's impediment It should be remembered that great players are great not through, but in spite of, any peculiarity of style.

The Model Player.

The earnest student is the model player. He is always quiet and unassuming in the company of other players, and generally before a concert gets into a quiet corner with his fiddle and scrapes away at some intricate passage not at all showy or pleasant to listen to, but of great benefit to his fingers or his violin. The strings, the instrument, and the player's fingers are thus prepared for what is to come. He works hard at home, and is not dainty in his selection of music, but will dig steadily into anything which he finds trying to his fingers or his bow. He thinks nothing of getting up in the morning two hours before other folks are out of bed, and scraping away at the severest of studies. Thus, when the slovenly and sleepy drone, who takes ten times as long as others to get out his fiddle and tune it, is staring in dismay at a new piece, your model player is quietly running his eye over the pages, noting the keys and the difficult passages, and he is thus ready to play it at sight, while the drone or the trifler can only make a wild scramble through. He is never taken by surprise, and he handles his violin not as if he were afraid of it, but as a man handles a spirited horse which he means to master. He is eager to learn every means by which his power can be extended and increased. He is not necessarily a clever or experienced player, but he is certain through time to be both. To him I give these hints, feeling assured that they will smooth his path and allow him to accomplish in a short time that which might not come with years of blind struggling Possibly the friendly poke in the ribs which I have administered to his less earnest brethren may rouse them to emulate his example, and not only read these hints but work them out.

Holding the Violin.

Many players are anxious to know which is the best chin-rest or violin-holder, and others as eagerly ask, "Is it necessary to use a chin-rest at all?" There is no best chin-rest, and whether a chin-rest is necessary depends upon circumstances Madame Neruda uses neither a chin-rest nor a shoulder-pad; yet a London dealer, in advertising his shoulder-pads, coolly declares that without them no lady can hold the violin properly. The time is fast approaching when advertiser and liar will be synonymous terms. Madame Neruda makes her shoulder her violin-rest—a favourite position with ladies. However, even that is not necessary in some cases Twenty years ago, I heard Mdlle. Bertha Brousil, of the Brousil Family, perform Hauser's "Bird in a Tree," violin solo, in the Music Hall, Edinburgh. This accomplished artiste wore an evening dress, and so could use no pad as a support to the violin; yet while tightening her bow, she did not take her violin from her chin, but held it there rigid and straight out, with the chin and collar bone alone, without the support of either the shoulder or the left hand. The position will be seen in the accompanying full-length figure, illustrating the power of the adjustable Spohr chin-rest. Whether a chin-rest is necessary depends upon the size of the player's collar bone, the build of the violin he uses, and the music he plays. If the collar bone be small, and not likely to develop, or if the player chooses to cover the collar bone over with an unwieldy pasteboard stiffened scarf, and thus keep out the violin, he had better have a chin-rest. Violins with bulging breasts, such as those of *Gaspard di Salo* and some of the *Amatis*, are exceedingly difficult to grip with the chin without the aid of a holder. Again, if the music performed be of a difficult and severe character, with much shifting and playing upon very high positions, a chin-rest will generally be an advantage, if not an absolute necessity. The shifting down of the hand without moving the violin is an easy matter with or without a chin-rest, but, as I have already shown, side slipping—that is, the sliding of the violin towards the right hand—demands a preventative, as in performing such a piece as Paganini's "Moto Perpetuo" there is absolutely not one moment from beginning to end during which the left hand is free to right the slip. I shall notice this piece more particularly in Chapter III., while treating of "Flexible Fingering."

The Spoon Chin-Rest.

The chin-rest known as the Joachim, which may be had for 2s. 6d., and the "Spoon Rest," shown in the accompanying engraving, which is a slight modification of the Joachim, and costs a shilling more, do not absolutely prevent side slipping, unless a pad or handkerchief be used along with the chin-rest.

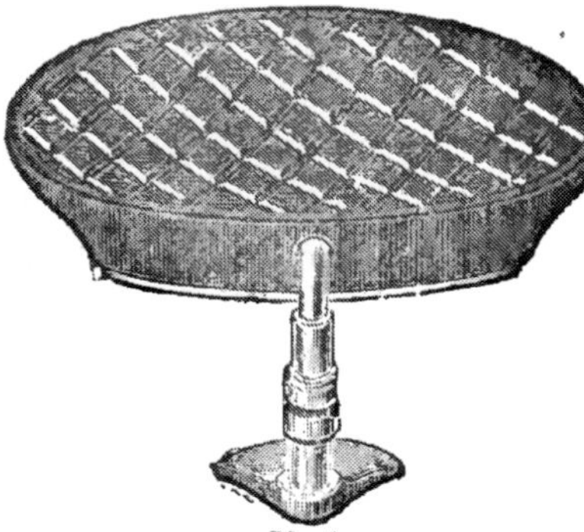

No 1.

The Double-ridge Chin-Rest.

The most popular chin-rest, and one which almost entirely prevents side slipping, is that made in the form shown in the engraving below.

It may be had with both ridges covered with velvet, and the rough surface of that velvet on the under ridge prevents side slipping. This under ridge also takes the place of a pad, and allows the head of the performer to be held higher. It is usually necessary to cut the velvet from underneath the ridges, except at the edge, so that they may rise clear of the breast and back of the violin, and touch the instrument only above the ribs. The objections to the velvet are, that it is often so badly dyed as to stain the shirt front, and so soon wears smooth and gets greasy, that it is necessary to renew the velvet. At my suggestion, the makers have therefore produced a double ridge

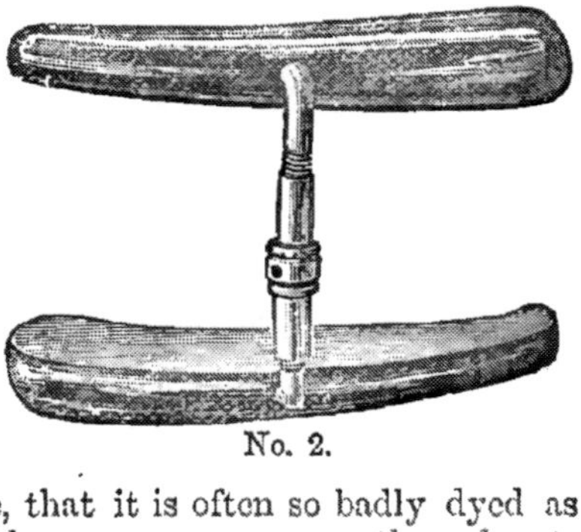

No. 2.

rest of the same model, with vulcanite ridges, carefully and closely serrated so as to give the indispensable roughness for preventing side slipping. The rest thus improved is cleanly and effectual, and needs no renewing of surface. Care has also been taken that the ridges rise clear of the breast and back of the violin except above the ribs, so that no cutting away is necessary to prevent muting of the tone; indeed, my impression is that this vulcanite rest, as well as No. 6, noticed further on, rather improves and gives compactness to the tone. This improved chin-rest, which is shown in the annexed engraving, has been named "The Professional Player's," and may be had from Messrs Köhler & Son, 11 North Bridge, price 3s., rough or smooth surface.

No. 3.

To prevent misapprehension, I may state that I have no interest whatever in the manufacture of these or any chin-rests, and the same remark applies to every thing recommended in this work.

The broader patch of the rest shown in the first engraving is chiefly recommended by the makers as a preservative to the breasts of old violins; and certainly if a violin had been very much broken and patched immediately underneath the chin, some such protector would be necessary.

The Spohr Adjustable Chin-Rest.

But the same end would be served, and additional advantages gained, by using the newly patented Adjustable Spohr Chin-Rest, made by Jenour Brothers, 49 Theobald's Road, London, of which, by the kindness of the patentee, I am enabled to give engravings below. What is possible with this chin-rest is shown in the first engraving. The position and feat is exactly that which I have noted as having been done by Mdlle. Brousil without either pad or chin-rest, but then every one is not a Brousil. I have tested the holder, and find that it is perfectly easy to accomplish the above apparently marvellous feat, with the holder adjusted as in the following engraving.—

No. 4.

The advantages of this position are that the plate of the chin-rest touches the violin only at one end; that the metal attachment is fixed on that part of the violin at which there is a solid block of wood underneath, and therefore is less likely to mute the tone or impede vibration, and that besides the excellent grip that is given, the violin is placed and kept at its proper slope for correct playing. There is real comfort in the hollow of the plate, which has been shaped with great care to the chin, and this plate may be had of diamonded wood or covered with velvet. It is the adjustable part of the holder, however, which will insure its adoption by many players. One may wish the plate as I have shown it, another might prefer one of the two following positions:—

No. 4.

Many men, many minds. The only objection to this chin-rest will probably be its appearance on the violin

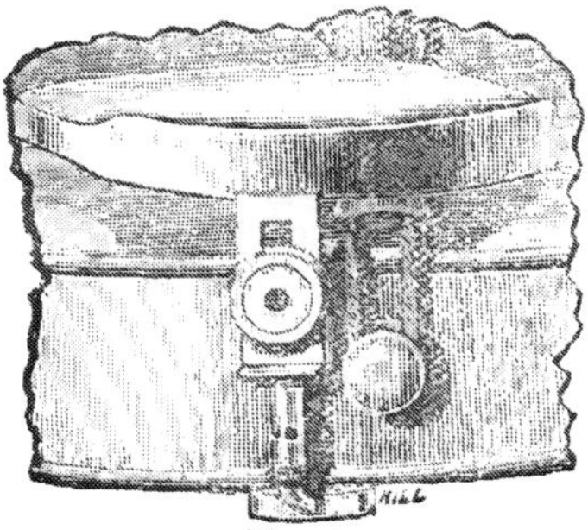

No. 4.

or its size. Most players who use a chin-rest are half-ashamed of it, and like it to be as small and unobtrusive as possible. The price is six shillings. For my own part, I should prefer the double narrow ridge vulcanite holder already noticed, to this or any that I have seen; but tastes differ widely.

Voigt's Chin-Rest.

Some may even consider the holding up of the violin by the left hand as an unnecessary labour and fatigue, and with a view to meeting their wants, the chin-rest next shown has been

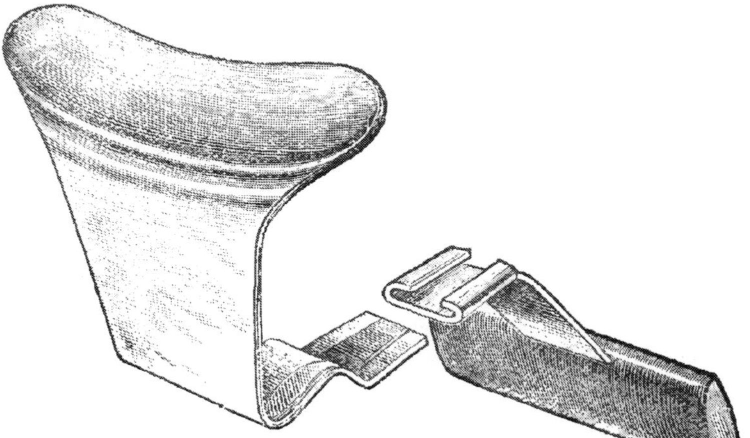

No. 5.

designed. It is named "Voigt's Violin Combined Chin and Shoulder Rest." By an ingenious arrangement for lengthening the plate, which here takes the place of the ordinary screw or screws, a kind of bracket, ending with a velvet-covered pad, is made to project from under the violin on to the left breast of the performer. It is an ungainly contrivance, but does prevent side-slipping, though the bracket is not acute enough to keep the violin horizontal, and the invention gives no more power in holding up the violin—as already shown in the full-length figure—than does the "Spohr Adjustable Chin-Rest." There is also an objection to this which applies to many violin chin-rests. In the strict school of violin playing, no movement of the body, or the chin, or the violin is allowed; nevertheless, even with the greatest of players, perfect rigidity is not possible, nor would it be graceful; and it is recovery from these elastic movements, and the righting of any minute slips of the violin, which are somewhat hampered by this elaborate bracketing arrangement of Voigt's. The design is of American manufacture; the metal part nickel plated; the chin-plate of polished black vulcanite; and the price is 7s. 6d. The makers are Messrs Alban Voigt & Co., 25 Edmund Place, Aldersgate Street, London.

The last chin-rest which I need notice is that represented in the engraving No. 6.

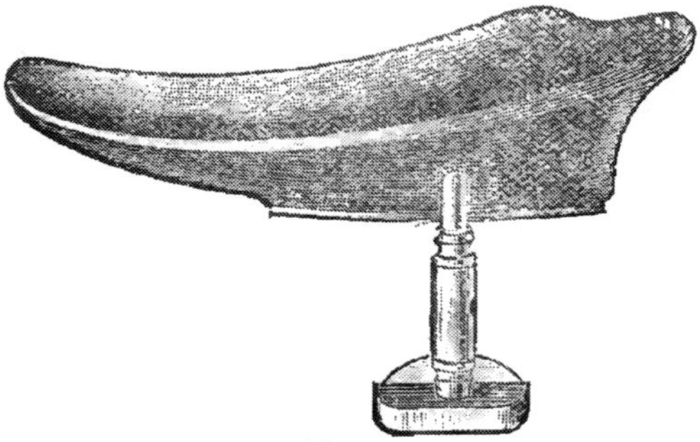

No. 6.

This is an exceedingly comfortable rest; rises clear of the violin breast over the greater part of its under surface; and does not mute, but rather improves the tone.

The chin plate is made of polished black-vulcanite, the screw of polished nickel silver, and the workmanship perfect. The price is 4s. The postage on any chin-rest is usually 2d. These rests may be ordered from the makers, or from Messrs Köhler

& Son, 11 North Bridge, Edinburgh, or through any musicseller. As the present work is sold by most musicsellers, I have affixed numbers to the illustrations, so that players sending from a distance may order by simply naming the number in the book.

One objection to all these chin-rests but No. 2 and No. 6, is that they do not allow of the violin being tucked *as far as possible* in under the chin. To some this may appear a trivial objection, but the thoughtful student—the really knowing and long-headed one—will, through time, discover that the nearer his left hand can be brought to his face, the more power he has in commanding the instrument. That is the true reason why the violin in the hands of all great artists appears such a small instrument—three inches at least of its broad end are

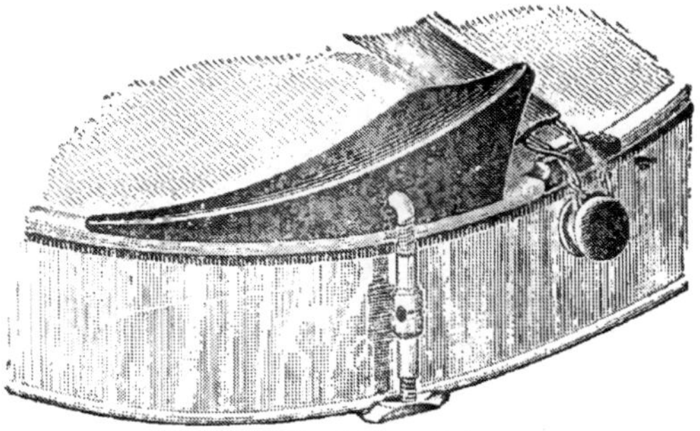

No. 6, fixed in position.

out of sight under the chin. Every eighth of an inch so hidden means so much power added to the execution with the left hand; every eighth of an inch which the chin is taken back, means so much hampering of the powers of the left hand. With the biggest patch that has yet been offered as a chin-rest, the chin, when in the hollow of the plate, is only one and a half inches over the ribs; there is thus a loss of at least an inch and a half, which is equal with some to playing upon a viola instead of a violin. A player with long arms and thin fingers, and fully three inches of the violin tucked out of sight under his chin, has no limit to his powers; the instrument is small—a mere "three-quarter" violin—to him. For this reason I most strongly recommend those violin-holders which place no limit upon the passing over of the chin on to the breast of the violin, namely No. 2 and No. 6. Of all holders which thus hamper the player, the *Joachim* is the worst; indeed, any player of average stretching powers may pass his chin completely over the plate of this holder, and rest it on the breast in front. Nor is the power so lost or gained confined to the left hand, for every eighth of an inch so lost or gained means the bow taken that much further away from the player, or brought that much nearer, and with that the power to draw it further in a straight line without either the turning over of the stick towards the player, or the quitting of the fourth finger.

Holding the Violin by the aid of No. 6 Chin-Rest only.

As to this last objection, let the student not make up his mind hastily, but for himself test the soundness of what I have here advanced, and be guided and influenced by the advice only if he finds that it is built upon a firm scientific basis.

CHAPTER II.

Holding the Violin—Variations of the Position of the Left Hand.

Having decided whether to use a chin rest or not, and how best to (1) keep the violin as nearly as possible horizontal, (2) at its proper slope towards the right hand for perfect and easy command of all the strings, and (3) to prevent it slipping either forward or to the side during any performance, however rapid or long continued, the player may consider the position and action of the thumb and fingers of the left hand.

In the frontispiece of the later editions of *The Violin: How to Master it*, I have given an engraving from a photograph, showing the position of the thumb on the neck of the violin thus—

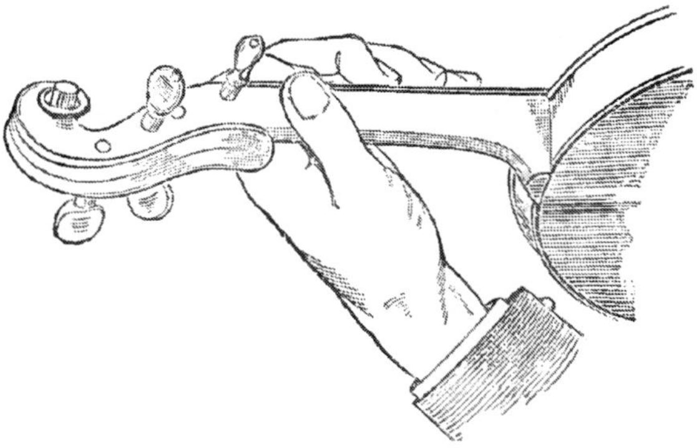

This may be named the Normal Position, and is correct for the performance of all music not of a very rapid nature. But when it comes to the performance of a study such as Paganini's "Moto Perpetuo," all in semiquavers, and requiring firm and rapid fingering, a stronger clasp on the neck of the violin is imperative, and the thumb is bent slightly at the first joint, so as to grip the neck more firmly. This may be named the Firm Position, and is shown in the following engraving:—

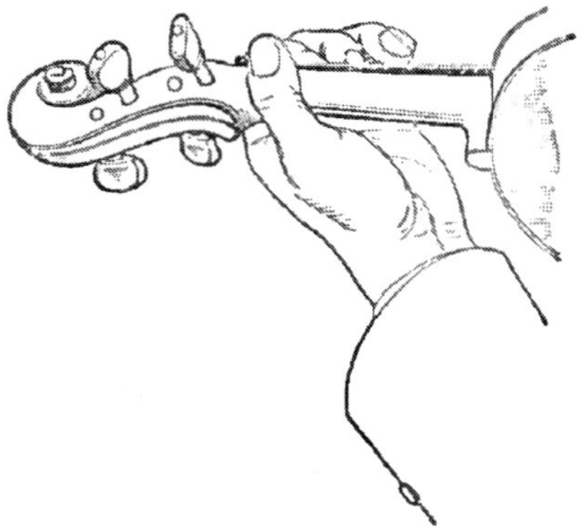

The thumb is really, on the first position at least, the sole guide and anchor of the whole hand, as any very strong pressure or grip with the bottom of the forefinger is to be deprecated. Through time, indeed, the player may, on the first position, perform many notes, shakes, and even short passages with the neck of the violin held solely by the thumb and the points of the fingers in use. This may be named the Free Position. Till the ability to do so is acquired, more especially with those who have not begun to play at a very early age, a good shake, close or open, on the first position, is almost an impossibility. The annexed engraving will illustrate this variation of the normal position, and shows the forefinger entirely free of contact with the neck of the violin.

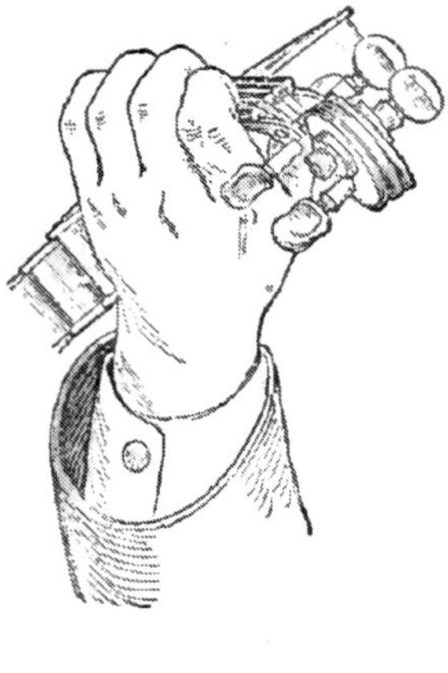

Many players realise through time that variations of the normal position are absolutely necessary to the execution of certain pieces of music, and instinctively adjust their hand to the changes; but some never understand them, and remain hampered for life, astonished and amazed at the execution of others, and at length despairingly attributing to superior ability that which only arises from superior knowledge.

The majority of the violin tutors only perpetuate the blunder, by at least implying that one rigid and immovable position of the left hand is to be adopted and adhered to.

The third modification of the normal position is one which is absolutely necessary of acquirement by all who desire to attain to really fine playing, and may be named the Anticipating Position. When a passage such as the following—

containing two rapid shifts on the fourth string, faces the student, to keep the thumb in the firm position already shown would surely hamper his execution of the run, if not make it impossible. He must with his thumb, from the first note, *anticipate* what is to follow, by bringing the hand well over the strings, and sinking the thumb further under the neck, as shown in the following illustration :—

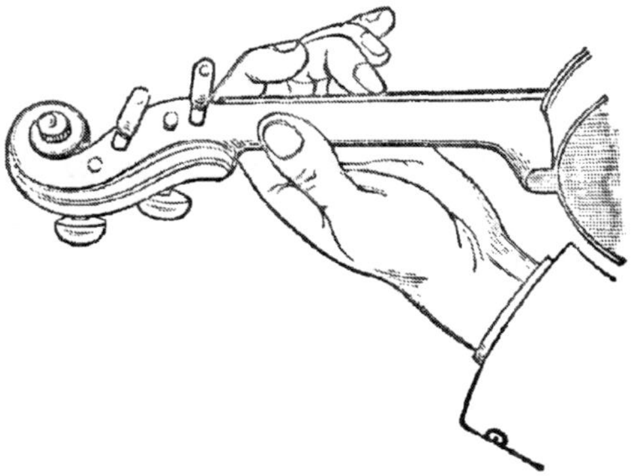

The reason for these variations—and there is a reason for everything in violin playing—is that the violin and strings being kept in a position almost rigid, cannot accommodate themselves to the hand and fingers of the player, therefore the hand and fingers must accommodate themselves to the violin and strings. The mountain will not come to Mahomet—Mahomet must go to the mountain. The ignorant player, indeed, will laboriously make the mountain come to Mahomet; and we frequently see him turn up the violin to a more acute angle when faced by a passage on the fourth string, and drop it back to rest again when the passage is finished, but that is mere fiddling, not violin playing. The violinist may move his body, his head, his arm, his hand, his fingers, his thumb, or even his feet and toes if he likes, but never the violin; that privilege is reserved solely for the fiddler and scraper.

In reality, the right way is always the easiest way. The left hand adjusts itself with the utmost facility to the above variations; and when they have been intelligently studied and mastered, the execution with the left hand is boundless. No passage finds the fingers unprepared, and a phrase which would be a terror to the mere fiddle-scraper never costs the "canning" one a thought. A little knowledge goes a great way; and the celebrated painter who attained such great results by "mixing his colours with brains" is a good model and example for the violin student.

CHAPTER III.

The Management of the Bow.

As in many other points of detail, the same rule will not apply rigidly to every one in the management of the bow. The principal rules I have already given in *The Violin: How to Master it* (page 35), and these will be found capable of almost universal application. They have been discovered, adopted, and almost reduced to a science by the greatest and best violin players of all times. Here and there, however, a new prophet starts up, and the student is puzzled and staggered by the strange utterances; but a thoughtful investigation, will generally demonstrate that the main principles laid down by all are the same. To draw the bow straight in a line parallel with the bridge, and to play with the hair turned on its outer edge, are the two points of good playing upon which every writer and teacher insists; how best to accomplish that acme of good playing the rules already alluded to will show. But on some minor points there must be a difference of opinion, as there are differences of hands, fingers, and arms. One writer says, that allowing the point of the little finger to quit the stick, when the extreme point of the bow is used, is to be regretted and deprecated. There are many things to be regretted in violin playing, but of two evils it is always best to choose the least. Those who are blessed with long arms and fingers will usually find that they can draw the bow to its point without this quitting of the little finger, and with only a slight turning over of the bow towards the player as it nears the point. One of our greatest players does so. But all are not so blessed, and all do not approve of this slight turning over of the bow at every long stroke, and the remedy of using a shorter bow is a poor one.

The Third Finger a Substitute for the Fourth.

Besides, when the little finger does quit the stick, it leaves the third finger to do its work. The palm of the point of the third finger is then pressed firmly upon the stick with the first joint slightly depressed, and the whole finger then acts as the balancer of the stick, in place of the fourth. The better to show the position while the bow is thus managed entirely with three fingers and the thumb, I have removed the hair and nut of the bow. In executing the upward stroke of the staccato bow, the above position and action of the fingers are imperative, as the strokes begin at the point and do not go past the middle of the bow; and so the fourth finger, with many hands, never gets a chance to resume its place as chief balancer. The fourth finger touches the stick except when the extreme point of the bow is being used, but the chief weight is borne by the third, as already described.

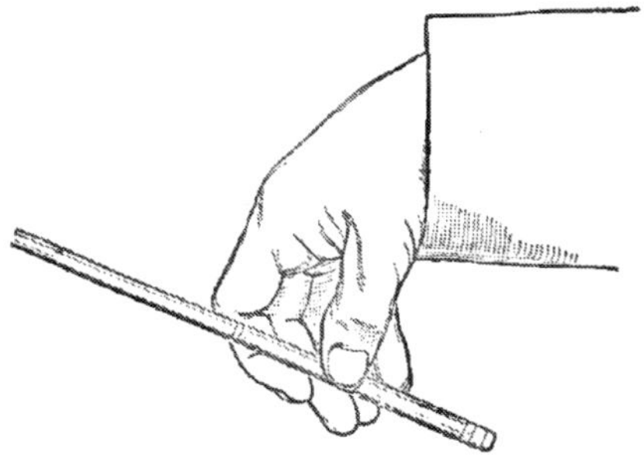

With the bow held thus, perfect command for any kind of stroke with the upper part is attained, and that without any tilting over of the stick towards the player, and consequent playing with the flat of the hair, or on its inner edge. With the majority of hands and arms, if this method be not adopted, and the fourth finger be kept supporting the stick during the passage of the entire length of the bow across the strings, a curve in the bowing is inevitable. The possible exceptional cases are where the player has long arms and long fingers with very flexible joints, and has begun to play in early childhood.

The Position of the Thumb.

It is not the extreme point of the thumb which presses the stick, but the palm of the point, inclined to the side. The point indeed is thrust through under the end of the hair till it almost meets and touches the point of the second finger coming round the stick from the opposite side Courvoisier recommends that part of the point should rest on the wood of the nut, which he wishes cut away for the purpose; but though this gives a certain degree of comfort to some thumbs, it has the drawback of seriously hampering the bowing by the hard ferule of the nut pressing the back of the nail, in place of the elastic hair. Any serious discomfort or pain in the thumb will usually be remedied by using the side of the palm instead of the tip as the point of pressure, and by substituting a soft bit of leather for the metal-covered thread usually wound round that part of the stick, which thread is often of base metal, and becomes corroded and poisonous.

The Left Hand—Flexible Fingering.

It is difficult to get the young, and more especially boys, to practise the violin steadily, and many parents give up the attempt with the words, "Wait till he is a little older, and knows the value of it." A little older generally means about the age of fourteen, and during the lapse of these years the muscles of the left hand which would have been split and set free have united and stiffened. To undo all that requires an amount of hard work and practice which are lamentable when it is considered how small an amount of daily practice during those seven or eight years, now for ever lost, would have prevented the evil. To find a player who has begun at the age of six—Madame Neruda performed solos in public at that age—is the exception; to find them beginning at the age of sixteen or even later is painfully common. Seeing, then, that the majority begin too late, their first study should be to find out the best means for most quickly undoing the mischief. The flexibility of finger and looseness of hand will never be quite so great as it would have been, by beginning young and keeping at the practice, but it will be very much greater than if none of the following means were tried, and certainly more quickly attained. The playing on the fourth string of severe studies and exercises, requiring firm fingering and far stretching—such as Campagnoli's "Four Studies in Monochord Playing" (price 3s 6d.; London. Cocks & Co, New Burlington Street), which after they are mastered may all be put on the fourth string—is a means of advancement, but too little known and understood even by professional players. The fourth string is most difficult of access; therefore, to constantly command its entire length, entails muscular exertion of the fingers, hand, and left arm, of the greatest benefit to the player, who will thus fit himself for feats on the other strings which would otherwise be impossible. Paganini understood this, and, notwithstanding his extraordinary length of finger and peculiarly thin and bony hand, forced himself to perform the most difficult studies which his brain could suggest, entirely on the fourth string. In a letter to a friend he said —

"A few weeks afterwards I produced a sonata on the fourth string, which I entitled 'Napoleon,' and executed it on the 25th of August before a large and brilliant audience. Its success far surpassed my expectation, and I may date from that period my predilection for the lower string; and as my audience never seemed to weary of the pieces I composed for it, I have at length arrived at that degree of facility which appears to have so much surprised you."

The practising of three octave scales and broken chords, such as those given in the appendix to Boosey's edition of "Spohr's Violin School," is another hand-loosener, which no advanced player can afford to neglect. These ought to be gone over at least twice a week, taking the run of three octaves in one bow, and giving no undue prominence or accent to any particular note in the scales.

Playing tenths on the violin is also a good stretcher for the fingers; and the shake exercises in Kreutzer's "Forty Studies for the Violin" have never been excelled for developing, surely if slowly, firmness and independence of fingering, but if the three exercises now to be described be taken along with these, the result will astonish the student.

Cork Stretching.

The first of these is finger-stretching with corks. Take three full-sized corks, and push one right up to the socket of each finger of the left hand, as shown in the following engraving:—

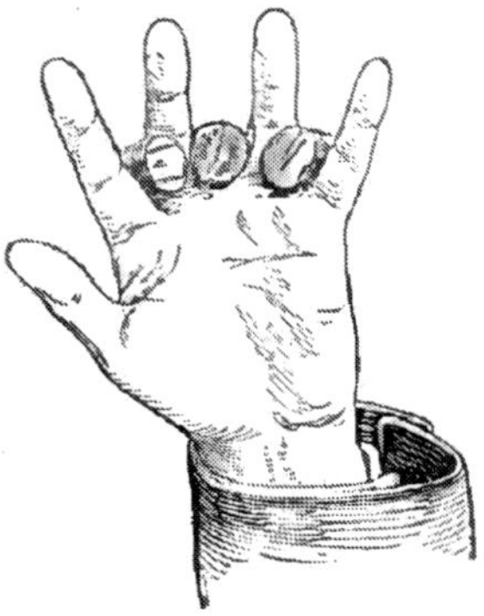

It is best to push in the centre cork last. The corks may at first be simply kept between the fingers for a few minutes, but after a little the player may practise shutting and opening his fingers, first together and then separately. If he cannot at first get the fingers to obey, he may help them in the exercise with his right hand. The effect of this cork practice is to split more deeply the muscles which control the fingers, which muscles are connected at the knuckles of the hand, and so to a certain extent prevent the fingers from acting independently of each other. How helpless most of us are in this respect, any one may prove by shutting his fingers, not the whole hand, firmly down on those fleshy cushions at their base, known in palmistry as the mounts of Jupiter, Saturn, the Sun, and Mercury, and then trying to extend the third or fourth finger without moving the others. Not one in a thousand can accomplish this apparently simple action, and the cause of failure is this connection of the muscles in the body of the hand. The cork-stretching, if practised for a short time daily, soon gives independence of action and flexibility of fingering, besides the ability to stretch easily the intervals required in the next study.

Finger-Stretching Exercise.

The second exercise is one of my own designing, and most students, when they first set eyes on it, are either appalled at the apparent difficulty, or led to bluntly declare that it is impossible of execution. "I don't believe it can be done—let me see you do it," has been more than once triumphantly levelled at me as an apparent clincher by students, who changed their

Finger-Stretching Exercises.

The Position.

Ex. 1.

Play each twelve times without stopping.

The Position.

Ex. 2.

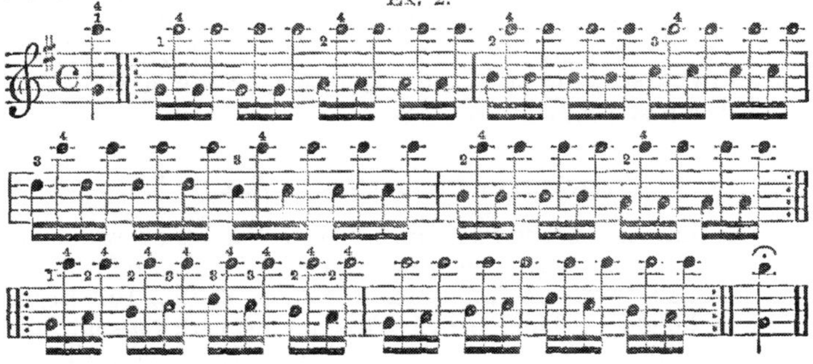

The Position.

Ex. 3.

tone very quickly, when I not only played it with ease, but in a moment or two transferred the power to them. The special bars at the beginning give the position of the first and fourth fingers on the strings, and the interval stretched is first a tenth, then an eleventh, and lastly a twelfth, which is equal to stretching a whole octave on one string. The intervening notes must be played with great distinctness, and the first and fourth fingers kept on the strings with great firmness, except in the third exercise, in which one lifting of the first finger is imperative To get the position the fourth finger must be placed upon the string first, and the first finger drawn back to its note afterwards If it will not come back, push it back with the point of the heel of the bow in the right hand, and having got it on the proper spot, keep it there. The exercises are of progressive difficulty, but even the last is not so stupendously difficult of execution as it may seem. In commanding the low notes, the first finger must be turned somewhat on its side. A little practice occasionally at this exercise will give great flexibility to the fingers and looseness to the whole hand, and make the stretching of an extra semitone, or even a whole tone, from the first position quite easy.

Paganini's "Perpetual Motion."

The third exercise is Paganini's "Moto Perpetuo," which may be had, with pianoforte accompaniment, for 1s 6d, of any musicseller, or direct from Messrs Schott & Co., 159 Regent Street, London. Though it is often performed as a solo, there is very little music in it. It is a mere trick piece to show rapid execution; but it is the best exercise for the violin ever written, whether it was really composed by Paganini or not. It is a kind of *Spinnlied,* written from beginning to end in semiquavers, modulates into a dozen different keys, and takes the hand on to every Position but the Second, from the First to the Ninth, with many stretched notes, to save shifting. It does not look difficult, and it really is not difficult until the proper speed is attempted, when its real nature is revealed To play it through should take less than five minutes, but he will be a smart player who, with a week's practice, can get through it in ten.

The real difficulty of the study lies in there being not a single pause or long resting note from the beginning to the end. The muscles of the left hand, however fatigued, get not the slightest pause to recruit or recover, but must exert themselves through the most rapid shifts and fingering, at the same break-neck speed till the last C is sounded. For this reason, when by slow degrees the piece has been mastered, it is much less fatiguing to play it at its proper speed in five minutes, than to take it slowly and occupy ten or fifteen; and until the proper speed is attained, the real musical meaning of the piece is never heard. It is the best exercise ever written for the violin, because (1) it is utterly impossible to play it through at its proper speed and hold either the violin or the left hand wrong; (2) it gives great agility and flexibility to the fingers; (3) it is excellent wrist practice for the right hand; (4) it compels firm fingering, that the rapid notes may not degenerate into a mere scuffle; and (5) though there is not a shake in it, it gives the power to make a good open shake. The study should be taken slowly at first, great care being exercised in the choice of fingering, as it is not easy to make after alterations; and the whole played with the upper half of the bow (held as shown in the illustration given at page 18), the *forte* passages at the middle, and the *piano* passages with the upper third part. If perfect command of the bow has been attained, the piece may all be played at the middle, the graduations of tone being entirely controlled by the pressure of the first finger It is to be played throughout in what may be named the "Rounded Staccato"—that is, the notes are neither to be "chopped," nor the bow taken from the string as in *staccato leggiero* The notes are played only a little sharper than if they were not marked with dots Crisp, clean, and neat would express the treatment of these notes better than staccato, and the hair of the bow rises a little, but does not entirely leave the string between each note. (For an explanation of the different meanings of the word *Staccato*, see *The Violin: How to Master it*, page 101) I append the fingering of some of the bars not amenable to the ordinary rules,—merely adding, that whenever a shift can be made on an open string, either ascending or descending, no pains should be spared to get at that open string for the purpose; and that when a shift or an awkward crossing from one string to another can be saved, or a blur avoided by stretching for a note, it must be done, even at the expense of a little delay in the mastering.

Moto Perpetuo.

Page 4, Bar 2.

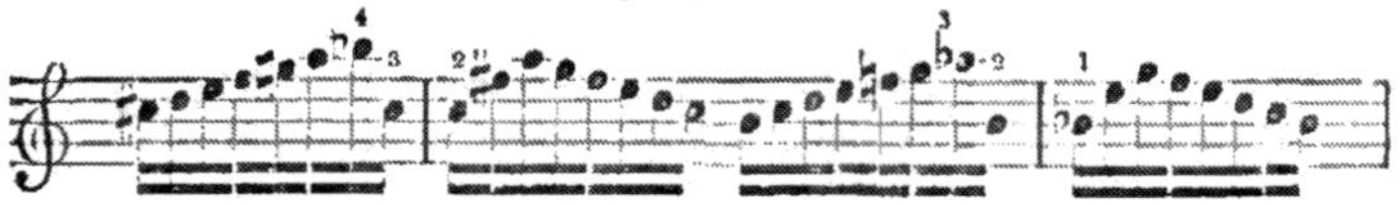

Page 5, Bar 16.

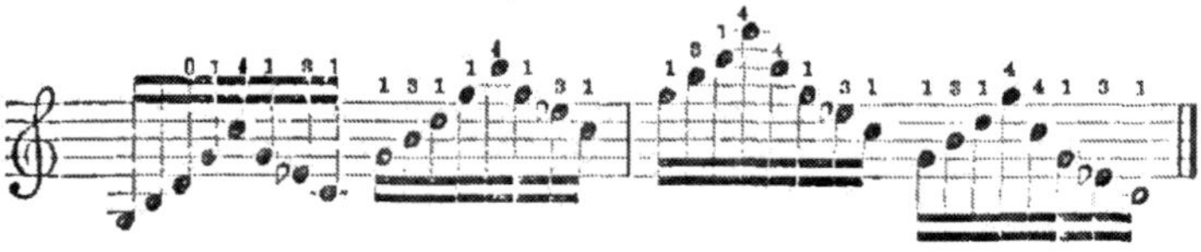

Page 6, Bar 21.

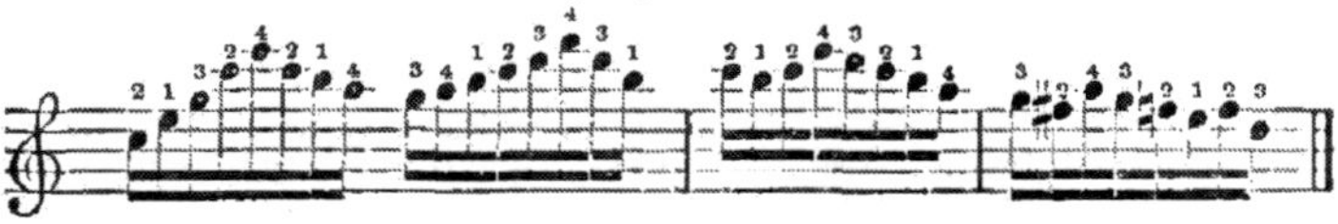

Page 6, Bar 24.

6th Position.

It is not an easy piece to get into the memory, so many of the phrases resemble each other, but by taking a page at a time, this may be accomplished, and the whole played right off without any stopping to turn over leaves. It is a capital study for any of those odd occasions when the student's leisure is limited to five or ten minutes, as it crams the greatest possible amount of "fatigue drill" into the time, which might otherwise be lost. When it is mastered it may easily be run through two or three times a day.

Stretching the Thumb.

Besides rendering the fingers flexible and independent, it is necessary to so stretch the fork of the thumb that the higher positions may be commanded with ease, however suddenly they may have to be attacked.

To allow the thumb to quit the neck of the violin entirely and rest on the ribs, is a desperate remedy, and one which should be adopted only when all other means have failed. The best stretcher for the thumb is playing steadily at any extemporised exercise far up on the fourth string, such as the following :—

Ex. 1.

The phrases within the dotted double bars may be repeated twenty times without stopping, and the first finger must be kept down with great firmness, to ensure of no moving of the hand after the position is gained. The whole of this exercise may be easily played without removing the thumb from the neck of the violin. If the thumb will *not* stretch to allow of the higher position being commanded, the following *arpeggio* for one string may be practised, putting it at first on the first string (E Major), and taking it gradually back till the fourth is reached.

Ex. 2.

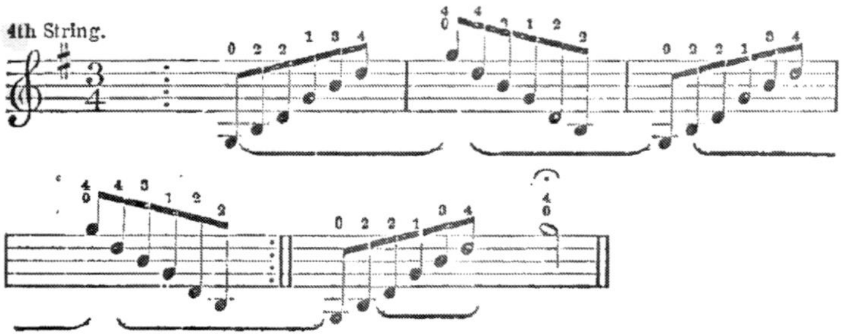

Ex. 3.

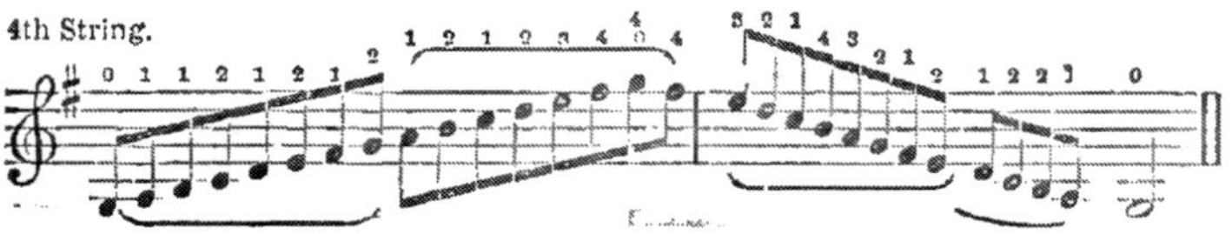

The notes may be played separately at first. The scale for one string which follows, is also an excellent stretcher for the thumb. Any player of average intelligence may invent dozens of these exercises for himself.

To steadily practise these gymnastics and studies, cannot fail to surely and rapidly develop the powers of the left hand.

CHAPTER IV.

How to Judge and Select Strings.

A good second or third string should be clear and transparent, quite smooth and round, and show none of the twists of the strands. When these strings are of a yellowish hue and opaque, and show the twists of the strands, they are old, and the tone will be dull and thick, even if they be put on a good violin. A good first string, whether it be rough or polished, should feel firm in the fingers, and when the fastenings of the coil are cut the string should bound out very much like a steel spring when set free. I prefer first strings also when they are transparent, but there are exceptions. If the string be white and opaque it will generally be a "screamer," and will not respond to any but the strongest pressure of the bow. If it has a limp, soft greasy feel in the fingers, and is also dull in its transparency, it will not be durable. If a string in being screwed up changes from transparent to opaque, it is bad, and the tone will be rusty if it does not snap before you can get it up to pitch. A string may be dull in its transparency (without the greasy softness), and yet be a capital string both for durability and tone. There is a polished Roman string of fine quality, usually sold at ninepence, which feels soft and velvety in the fingers, but which is delightful in tone, though somewhat weak and soft. This string is clear as glass, and pretty durable.

A string, resembling this closely, is made and sold by J. Edwin Bonn, Brading, Isle of Wight, under the name of the "Premier Violin String" It lies limp and inert when the coils are set free, instead of having that fine spring, which is generally a sign of a brilliant tone, and like most severely polished strings, a good deal of the soul has been ground out of it It is a pretty string to look at, and that is about all that can be said about it. The price is ninepence for one string of three lengths.

A first string, which goes up to pitch with but a few turns of the peg, will generally be durable. The first string is the most important, as it is apt to break at an awkward moment, therefore the player should not rest till he discovers some dealer who can supply him with exactly the string he needs, and then keep by that string and that dealer. Distance need be no drawback, as the penny post has brought all places near.

Violin strings should never be oiled after they come from the maker. Oiling dulls the tone, rots the string, and makes the missing of notes in *piano* passages almost certain. 'Cello strings, however, which last longer, being so much thicker, are sometimes improved by being taken off the 'cello, oiled lightly, wiped dry, and allowed to "rest" for a night before being put on again. Italian strings are best (and dearest), as they are mostly made and dried in the open air German strings, partly made and dried in the open air, come next; and English strings, made and dried entirely within doors, come last. Of Italian strings those made at Naples are considered best, those at Rome next, and those at Padua third best I always get my first strings (rough Neapolitans, 8s 6d per bundle of 30), from Mr. Edwin Race, St John's, Isle of Man. They are generally good, and certainly cheap. For Seconds and Thirds I find none better than those sold by Mr. D. L. Thompson, 134 Nethergate, Dundee, 6d. each (two lengths). The same dealer sells particularly soft-toned silver Fourths, at 1s 6d. each. A more brilliant toned Fourth, of Florence silver, with silk between the gut and the wire, may be had of Mr. Ed. Withers, Wardour Street, London, price 1s. 9d.

Every violin player should keep a string gauge carefully marked at the exact spots for the sizes of the strings he uses, and use it constantly in selecting strings, as the eye is easily deceived. This applies more particularly to the second, third, and fourth strings, which must be gauged so as to give perfect fifths at any part of the strings. Sometimes a string, which is out of balance with the rest, may be put right by being reversed. The third and fourth are the most difficult to be got to agree perfectly in fingering.

In sending to a distance for strings, with a specimen size, it should be borne in mind that a string gets slightly thinner by being strained on the violin for months. This stretching and thinning often make a string so much out of balance with its fellows, that is, make the fingering get so much closer on the first position, that true fifths are impossible, and the string has to be taken off This is particularly the case with the third and the second strings. The fourth does not alter much, and the first seldom lasts long enough to be severely tried in this particular The third is almost certain to get out of balance with the fourth before it is worn done Reversing the string might remedy the evil, but a string which has been fingered has always a rusty tone when reversed. The only alternative, then, is to change the string, as it is difficult to finger one string flatter than its fellows, particularly in playing chords, and in playing fifths, where but one finger can be used, it is absolutely impossible.

Mr Thompson's strings cannot be called cheap, but they are exceptionally fine in tone; and as the second, third, and fourth strings do not need to be renewed so often as the first, the difference in the price is trifling in the long run "Tested strings" may be bought in sets from the principal London dealers. They are very dear (1s. 6d each, I think), but are warranted to play perfect fifths—that is, the fingering is warranted to be the same on every string. They are also warranted durable, but the one given me to test did not stand well. The string which is absolutely reliable has yet to be discovered, and a fine string often goes quickest. A "screamer," or one which plays false, generally lasts intolerably long. The tone of these tested strings is exceptionally clear, pure, and fine, and it ought to be, at the price. Tested strings are polished, and polishing a string must always wear down some of the strands, and so weaken the string. However, each player must consult his own liking and his own purse. The majority of professional players prefer the rough or unpolished string for the first. It is thought to be truer, to bite better, and to have more life in it, which means more than mere durability. When wanted for a solo, however, the rough string should be put on a day or two before, and ground down a little by practice. This also prevents the annoyance of the string sinking much during the performance, and is preferable to putting on a new string on the day on which it is to be used, and tugging all the stretch out of it. Tugging thus at a new string pulls a good deal of the tone out of it. A string which has not been tugged, but simply kept up to pitch and played upon for days, till it seems almost worn through, will often last through a whole night's hard playing better than a new string put on specially for the concert. Thus the strings of amateurs, though probably the best that can be had, and put on only an hour before the concert, go snap, snapping all the evening, while the professional player looks on with a smile. He has prepared his string days before, or let the old one take its chance, after a careful inspection and calculation. He is cooler too, of course, and goes to his fiddling as unconcernedly as the amateur goes to his workshop or his desk, and that coolness saves the string a little. He knows where to buy his strings too, and knows exactly what the strings he always uses will do, and never asks them to do more. In nearly every town, there are to be found stationers' or ironmongers' shops in which violin strings are sold The owners of these shops know nothing about strings, but buy them as they would buy drugs, or tea, or anything out of their line. In such places the strings are often put into the window or a glass case to tempt buyers, as a grocer would display sugar, till all the soul is sunned out of them. When that has been accomplished, and the strings are plainly shouting out "I'm dead! I'm rotten! don't buy me!" they may be brightened up with a dose of oil, and put back into the box to be palmed upon the first buyer. No one of experience would buy strings from such places. It is worse than throwing money away. The dealer from whom you buy your strings, whether he be a string importer, a musicseller, or a stationer, ought to have (first and most important) a great sale, (second) he ought to know where to get good strings, and (third) he ought to know how to keep the strings while they are in his possession. Strings will keep good for a whole year, and even improve in tone and durability, if kept in a closely shut tin box, in a cool dry place, excluded from sun and air, with no grease or oil on the paper which covers them.

For a month or two after being made, violin strings are somewhat raw, and do not last well. After being kept as described above for a time they harden and firm, and are better in tone and more durable. In nearly every large town there is at least one musicseller or dealer who keeps good strings, and it is best to find out one of these, and send to him always. Many send to London for their strings, but there is often nothing great about the strings but the price. If cheapness be not an object, however, the player who prefers to deal with a London house should always buy from a firm of established repute, such as Edward Withers, or Hart, or Hill & Sons, all of Wardour Street, who make a specialty of high-class violin strings, and sell such quantities that the strings may reasonably be expected to be both good and fresh.

The Points of a Good String.

To sum up, a good string is to be known (1) by its appearance and hue, (2) by its spring when the coils are set free, (3) by its feel in the fingers (if too soft and limp it will not be durable, if too dry and hard it will be a "screamer"), and (4) by its not showing decay, and the windings of the strands. Sometimes strings have a suspicious look, and turn out good; but it is more common to find them look well and turn out bad. A finer tone is always to be got out of strings selected rather thin than thick. Some of the old violins of high build must have the thinnest strings that can be got, or they will sound "tubby." The tone is also clearer, and less inclined to huskiness than with thick strings. By attending to these hints a player may soon know a good string, and will be able to tell almost exactly the kind of tone it will produce when put on the violin.

The Fourth String.

The back strings last so long that it is not necessary or advisable to keep many of them by you. Keep by you any old or common Fourth string, in case of a sudden breakage. The Fourth you use should always be as fresh as possible when put on, as this string is apt to shrink in its metal covering, and rattle disagreeably. A rattling Fourth may sometimes be cured by taking it off the violin and letting it rest for a few weeks. When put on again the rattle is gone. There are great varieties of silver-covered Fourths, some quite as coarse in tone as any twopenny copper one; others ringing and "gritty"; others smooth and soft Some violins sound best with a copper Fourth; others with a soft-toned silver one; others with a brilliant-toned silver one. Some players do not like a Fourth string without a certain amount of "grit" in it, and always make the grit heard when they play upon that string. I shall notice this more particularly in the chapter on "Tone—Forced and Developed" My own idea is that there should be as little difference as possible in the tone when running on to the Fourth string. The Fourth certainly differs in character from the others, and for that reason has whole passages and pieces specially arranged for it, but that has nothing to do with "grit" My meaning is, that when a passage is played upon both third and fourth strings—such as the *Adagio* in De Beriot's Fifth Air—the tone on the Fourth string should be as soft and smooth and sweet as on any part of the third, and that while performing such a passage it is defective art to allow any appreciable difference to strike the ear. Even with a soft-toned Fourth, the pressure must be diminished, or the bow taken further from the bridge, to accomplish that result. To jar, or rasp, or "bite," on the Fourth string at any time is vile, and quite unpardonable with any string The Fourth string being more difficult to get into vibration, should be coaxed and wheedled and caressed, not torn at tooth and nail. Most especially with this string should the bow be so handled that the violin "shall seem to breathe the first tone it gives." (See *The Violin: How to Master it*, page 48.) And should one so practise as to not be able to play a gritty *sforzando* note? Well, any one can do that. Put a violin into the hands of a perfect novice, and he will play such a note, with no practice or training at all. It is easily done—only too easily—the difficulty is not to do it. Many solo players, otherwise excellent, attack the fourth string as if they had a long standing grudge against it, and were eager for revenge. It is like saluting one's lady love with a blow instead of a gentle kiss.

Preparing Strings for Solo Playing.

When about to play a solo, should you be forced to put on new strings, or wish to do so for the fresh and fine tone, play upon them diligently for three or four days, so as to wear the round face of the string somewhat flat. This wearing and smoothing must be carried right up to the bridge, so that even at that part no scratchy note may suddenly mar the beauty of the tone. The close shake is always got stronger by playing with the hair of the bow brought near the bridge, and there are other reasons for having that part of the string prepared, to which I shall allude in the chapter on "Tone—Forced and Developed;" but here it may be affirmed that the fullest and finest tone is never got out of the violin until the strings are thus worn flat in the face. Even the metal-covered fourth, though it cannot be flattened much in the face, is improved by being played upon from the top of the finger-board close up to the bridge.

In stringing the violin great difficulty is sometimes experienced in getting hold of the end of the second string after it is passed through the hole in the peg, on account of that peg being so far in beneath the scroll of the violin. At page 34 of *The Violin: How to Master it*, I have given

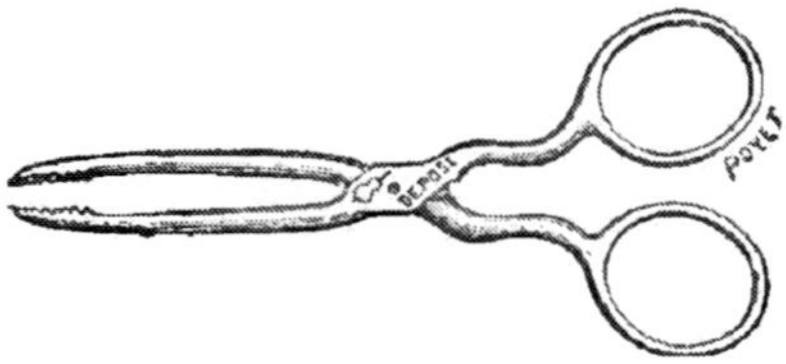

the best method of getting over the difficulty unaided; but with some violins this will fail, and players thus troubled frequently are forced to keep a loop of gut constantly attached to that peg, which is untidy and apt to break. The new "A" string catcher, brought out by Messrs Lafleur & Son, 15 Green Street, Leicester Square, London, the engraving of which is here given, will relieve the violin player of all anxiety on that account. The contrivance is of polished steel, and somewhat resembles a pair of neat pocket scissors wedded to a pair of pliers. The serrated teeth fit into each other closely to the very point, and give a sure grip. The price is 1s. 8d., post free.

Fine Rosin for Solo Playing.

In the appendix to *The Violin: How to Master it*, there will be found an excellent recipe for fine rosin. In preparing violin rosin, however, great care is necessary, as the slightest over-heating of the mixture in melting will render the rosin hard and brittle. Hard rosin gives a harsh tone, and flies too soon from the hair. It is also apt to collect at the side of the strings, and under a heavy pressure of the bow give a grating tone almost unbearable, the only remedy being to scrape off the accumulation with the back of a penknife. Rosin too soft, gets greasy and sticky; and there are some localities near the sea, where the air is heavily impregnated with saline particles, which are a perfect distraction to the violin player, from the manner in which they render the best of rosin sticky and useless. It follows, therefore, that the same rosin will neither suit every player nor every place. For fine playing, the nearest approach to that of which I have given the recipe are the cakes prepared by Gand and Bernardel, Paris, price 6d, and by Otto Schuster, which are wrapped in red leather, inside the box, price 6d. The latter is just crisp enough, and is therefore best suited for orchestral playing. So sensitive is this material that no two cakes are ever alike, and it might be necessary to go over a dozen, even by the same maker, before one of the desired degree of fineness be discovered. A number of attempts have lately been made to put up violin rosin in a handy and cleanly form for use, such as placing the rosin on a metal bobbin, with high edges to prevent the hair slipping over during the application, or like the "Acme," within the boards of a miniature china book, but unluckily the ingenuity of the inventors seems to be entirely expended upon the case or holder of the rosin, whereas it is the compounding of the rosin itself which should call for the most profound study. The price of all these prepared boxes is out of all proportion to the cost, and to charge 1s. or 1s 6d. for a small square of rosin, which costs about the twentieth of a penny, seems to me simply robbery in disguise. For a few pence enough rosin to last a lifetime may be prepared, by the recipe I have given, care being taken not to overheat the mixture.

Improved Violin Mute.

The use of the mute is to be deprecated in all but those orchestral works in which the *sourdine* effect is demanded. Every violin player, however, must have a mute, and he may as well have the best that has been designed—that made by Messrs Wm. E. Hill & Sons, Wardour Street, London. This invention is neatly made of vulcanite, and its recommendations are that it can be put on noiselessly; does not mark the bridge; never gives the burring or nasal sound peculiar to all other mutes under a strong pressure of the bow, and altogether gives a more legitimate, or violin like, tone, than the old metal mute. The price is 1s.

CHAPTER V.

Adjusting the Violin.

Most of the rare old violins are like the more gifted of mankind—sensitive, "cranky," irritable. They take offence easily; get out of order without any apparent cause; rebel altogether at times. One will refuse to except any change of bridge or alteration of sound-post, and will stick to the point till it conquers Others, particularly the *Guarnerius*, will resent neglect by becoming hoarse-voiced, and will only allow the resentment and malady to thaw under diligent practice. Even with every attention, and with no important alteration in the adjustment, they will at times take a fit of the dumps, and scarcely allow themselves to be coaxed back into good humour. Very often they will resent even the putting on of a new string, and become reconciled only after a day or two's hard playing. The best cure for these fits is to take no notice of them—play away as usual, and let the freak evaporate. The player should always be master, and make the mastery felt. Very often a trifling alteration in the adjustment is all that is wanted to effect a marvellous cure. Skill in adjusting a violin only comes after many years to the violin player The chief requisites are a sharp ear, patience, and a certain neat-handedness which is inborn with many. Many experiments in adjusting a violin should not be made at a time, as the ear becomes tired, and less sensible to the changes effected in the tone. Adjustment so far as the violin player is concerned, is limited to three things—the bridge, the sound-post, and the strings; but by the aid of a violin maker it may be extended to other three—the bass-bar, the re-setting of the neck and finger-board, and lining, or what Charles Reade calls "sandwiching," the thin or worn portions of the back or breast. We may notice these in the order given above.

The Bridge.

No rule can be given for the shape or thickness of the bridge Experiment alone can decide for the player what kind of bridge suits his violin and suits *him*. Some bridges are made with the feet thick and wide apart, others with the feet small and closer together. The general rule as to the width of the feet is that it is governed by the position of the sound-post and bass-bar, the back edge of the centre of the right foot of the bridge to be immediately in front of the front edge of the sound-post; and the left foot to be immediately above the centre of the bass-bar. The feet of the bridge should always be sloped, and fitted to the bulge on the breast of the violin, as carefully as the ends of the sound-post are fitted to the slopes of breast and back inside. In many old violins the breast is indented forward in the direction of the pull of the strings through the carelessness of former owners in not keeping the bridge perpendicular. In such a case, if a straight-footed bridge were put on just as it came from the maker, it would always tend to hang forward. The feet must be sloped to fit the indentation, by being ground down behind with a file. They must be adjusted to the bulge on the breast also, so as to press on the breast equally with every part of the feet while standing perpendicular. Rough or unpolished strings tend to pull the bridge forward, and it is advisable to hold the top of the bridge back with the left hand while screwing up a new rough string for the first time. It saves trouble and prevents accidents A violin which is hard in tone ought to have a bridge of soft wood, and rather thin than thick, and a sound-post of soft pine. A violin which is soft in tone may be made more brilliant by putting on a bridge of hard wood, and inserting a sound-post of hard pine. If one string or two strings be thick and unwieldy in tone, the defect may be removed or modified by thinning the bridge at that side with a file or emery paper. If the build of the violin be high, and more especially if the breast and back are rounded outwards towards the edges instead of hollow, the tone will probably be hard, but may be clear and penetrating by way of compensation. This hardness may be modified by refitting the violin with a deep bass-bar of soft pine, and by stringing with thin strings. No violin which is hard in the tone will endure thick strings. A violin which is what is called "tubby" in tone—that is, deep and hollow in tone as well as hard—may often be entirely cured by stringing it with thin strings, keeping the sound-post well back from the bridge, and putting on a thin bridge and a new and deeper bass-bar of soft pine. Thus treated, the former dreadful qualities are changed into actual beauties; the loud loose tone is compressed into a clear brilliant one, which carries well, and responds instantly. It is a trick quite unworthy a genuine violin player to put on a string thick in proportion to the others, to give more tone to a string weaker than its fellows, for by so doing the balance of the strings is upset, and pure cords, octaves and fifths, are an impossibility, as the fingering of that string is different from that on the others. So also is the trick of leaving the bridge slightly higher at a string which is weaker in tone than its fellows. These tricks are regularly practised by dealers in high-priced instruments, to conceal their weak points, and are seldom detected until the instrument is bought and more closely tested. The bridge should be carefully rounded to the lie of the finger-board, leaving it rather lower at the first string. This may be tested by putting on the bridge before it is finally smoothed off, and looking along the finger-board from the scroll end. When the proper shape and fit of feet and top are got, the top is to be smoothed off with fine emery paper, being left rather round than sharp. Four very slight indentations may then be made at the proper place for each string by rubbing the back of a knife across the edge of the bridge. The pressure of the strings will soon deepen and harden these; notches with a knife are not so good. The first and second strings are generally kept rather closer to each other than the others.

The Sound-Post.

The same rule may be followed with the sound-post as the bridge. If the tone of the violin be hard, let the sound-post be of soft pine, not too thick, and not streaky—that is, not having veins or layers of resin running through it. If the tone be too soft, let the sound-post be of hard pine and streaky. Old wood is best, but the same rule holds good, however old the wood I had a sound-post sent me from Russia, which was made out of part of a pine table at least 200 years old. I eagerly hastened to insert it in my violin, but found the tone too hard, and had to take it out and restore the old one. Hardness of tone may also be modified by keeping the sound-post a little back from the foot of the bridge—say a quarter of an inch behind.

Inequality of tone may be modified, and sometimes entirely cured, by altering the position of the sound-post thus:—If the first and second strings be weak, bring the sound-post nearer the *f* hole at that side; if the third and fourth strings be weak, let the post be placed nearer the bass-bar. If the tone be wished louder all over, bring the sound-post more directly under the right foot of the bridge—say with its front edge a sixteenth of an inch under the back edge of the foot. This will give more tone, but the quality will not be so good. Pushing the sound-post nearer the bass-bar often necessitates the making of a new post a slight degree longer, as the distance is increased between back and breast. Bringing it nearer the right *f* hole, in like manner often necessitates the shortening of the post, so that the post may not fit too tightly or bulge the breast of the violin. The post should just fit easily, top and bottom, without the pressure of the strings. If it be too tight, the tone is never so good, especially if the violin be old and fine; if it be too slack, the least jerk will bring it down, and endless trouble will follow.

As already noticed in *The Violin: How to Master it*, the ends of the post must be very carefully sloped to fit the bulge of back and breast, and in adjusting these it is sometimes necessary to take out the tail-piece peg at the head of the violin, and look into the violin in a strong light, to see that these ends fit closely all over their end surfaces, and also to ascertain if the post stands perfectly perpendicular.

The sound-post is the most irritating, cranky, delightful, tormenting little demon in the whole violin. Sometimes the right spot for it may be hit upon in a moment, as by inspiration; at others hours of sweating and excitement, patient toil, and agonising suspense have to be expended before the desired result is attained. In testing and adjusting, the post may be moved back or forward without slackening the strings, by tapping it gently, top and bottom, with the handle of a table-spoon, or drawn to right or left with the hooked end of the sound-post setter. How to make a simple sound-post setter, I have already described at p. 32 of *The Violin: How to Master it* The sound-post is sometimes set with the grain crossing that of the breast of the violin, lest the one should indent the other, but that, I think, is putting too fine a point on adjustment. When the right spot is discovered, it should be marked by drawing a pen or pencil round the end of the sound-post touching the back of the violin. That precaution makes the readjustment, in case of an accident, an easy matter.

The Bass-Bar.

In the adjustment of an old violin to the modern requirements of raised concert pitch and high shifting, the bass-bar plays an important part; but on this point, as a mere player and not maker of the violin, I have little to say. All the old Italian and other violins by makers of celebrity have had new bass-bars inserted. The amateur violin maker generally has a craze, and that craze is often in connection with the shape or size, or thickness or length, or position of the bass-bar. These monomaniacs ought to be kept at arms' length. I met one once, who declared that he could make any violin superior in tone by placing the bass-bar so as to run from the usual place at the left foot of the bridge across to the opposite corner, so as to pass under the finger-board. Another I have heard of, who shapes the bass-bar like a crescent moon; and others, who hint darkly at some mysterious system or method which they have discovered, and practise, but which they refuse to speak of or reveal As imagination flourishes as strongly among violin players as among the patrons of quack medicines, these men have generally numerous testimonials certifying the perfect success of their labours. They are generally chock-full of theories as to sound waves, tones, centres of vibration, &c; but in violin making an ounce of practical skill is worth a ton of theory. The best professional makers and repairers of violins have now fixed rules upon which they work in the adjustment of bass-bars to particular models of the violin; and if the violin be a valuable one, it is always safest to entrust the insertion of a new bass-bar to one of these, rather than to an amateur, full of brand new theories. If the violin be not a valuable one—that is, if it be poor and coarse in tone—all the cranky bass-bars in the world will never make it other than the wretched thing it is.

The Neck and Finger-Board.

Accompanying the insertion of a new bass-bar in a really valuable old violin there is generally the setting back of the neck to increase the pressure on the breast and allow of the high positions being more easily commanded by the left hand. This is generally done by the insertion of a new neck neatly joined to the old scroll. No really skilled violin maker would dream of any other method, but I have been told of a violin maker in Aberdeen who adopted the brutal expedient of sawing a slit in the neck, sloping downwards from that part under the finger-board at which it is joined to the body of the violin, and then when the cut was deep enough, hammering in a wedge of wood covered with glue, which he then dressed off and varnished. That man must have descended from the Goths and Vandals. It must have been a relation or ancestor of this maker who discovered the cheap expedient of raising the finger-board by inserting under it a thin wedge of wood, without setting back the neck at all. This allows the use of a higher bridge, which always gives more tone, though at the expense of the quality; but it increases the difficulty of commanding the high positions. It also makes the violin more heavy upon strings.

Sandwiching.

But of all barbarous expedients in the renovating of old violins, none is worse than that of sandwiching. Very often in hearing a genuine *Cremona* played upon, while admiring the rich quality of the tone, a suspicion creeps upon the listener which he seldom dares to express. On a particular string—or possibly on more than one—the tone seems a little husky, as if a hair were fizzing against the string or along with it. It is but seldom that the prejudiced owner will admit the existence of the defect. "It is all imagination," he will declare, or the critic is "finically acute." But if the existence of the huskiness be admitted, and traced to its source, in the majority of cases the cause will be found to be "sandwiching"; that is, the strengthening or thickening of the breast or back of the violin by gluing on a thin layer of wood inside. I am willing to believe in many cases it was sandwiching or no violin—that the instrument was so broken or worn, or had been so ignorantly scraped or thinned, that without the layer of wood it would have been simply a curiosity for a glass case, and for ever laid aside from use but I am as certain that many violins have been so treated which would have been far better without it. Very often a few cracks make a breast or back look to the repairer ominously weak and near the sound-post Glue, he thinks, will scarcely stand the pressure; and lo! to make sure, he claps on a broad patch of wood smoothly over all, very often —oh, the wretch!—scooping out a nicely fitting hollow for the new wood in the old breast The thing is done, and done for ever. No tears of the owner, or protests or regrets, will ever undo that clever "restoration" The violin is stronger certainly; but the tone!—it is like a fine voice after an attack of diphtheria—probably husky for ever. Now, in a case like this, I should say to the repairer, have every faith in the power of glue alone. If properly applied, and the finest that can be had, it will often hold more firmly than the fibres of the wood, so that we frequently see a new crack made by an accident, close to an old glued one which has not yielded. Then, if it positively will not stand, let the cracks be bound across with tiny straps of wood rather than a wholesale sandwich. This will give at least a portion of the injured wood liberty to vibrate freely, and the huskiness will be all but imperceptible. About fifty years ago some clever fellow, upon whose grave the "cursory remarks" of connoisseurs and violin players now rest somewhat heavily, announced that the breasts of the old violins were too thick of wood, and were mightily improved in resonance by being scraped thin. Many owners of the real gems caught the craze, and their violins were thinned down and for ever injured A violin scraped down thus certainly vibrates more easily, but the tone is hollow and spurious, and does not carry well; besides which, the violin deteriorates steadily, instead of improving. Most of these spoiled instruments have been sandwiched, but of course the tone will never be comparable with that of violins not so injured and repaired,—it merely shows the remains of beauty once admired, and is good for nothing but to extract tears of regret and "cursory remarks."

The Pegs.

There is a great difference in the attitudes here shown—the one is clumsy and vulgar, the other graceful and easy. The one shows the player tuning without having the strings properly adjusted on the pegs, the other with the pegs so locked with the strings that they never slip, and that all four may be tuned without lateral pressure. The method I have already explained at page 33 of *The Violin: How to Master it* (price 1s. Edinburgh: Messrs. E. Köhler & Son, 11 North Bridge). Very fine pegs of dark brown rosewood, which work very smoothly, and are delightfully comfortable to the fingers, may be had of Messrs. Hill & Sons, 38 New Bond Street, London, price 2s. per set. Next to these are pegs of boxwood, dyed black, which work well and do not split like those of ebony. The hole in the peg should never lie much over $\frac{1}{8}$ of an inch from the side of the box or it will not lock easily with the string. When it has worked in much over that distance a new hole must be drilled in the peg. A peg which sticks in its socket may be made to work smoothly by applying a mixture of chalk and black lead.

Jerking of the pegs is caused by the socket of the peg, or the peg itself, not fitting smoothly all round. The remedy is to smooth out the socket with fine emery paper glued round an old peg, and then work in a new peg with black lead till both peg and socket at the parts in contact show a surface glossy and smooth as glass all round. A little attention and patience in this matter will save years of irritation.

The Peg Turner.

A peg will at times get so locked in its socket that the strongest fingers cannot move it back or forward without the help of a pair of pliers. This usually arises from carelessness in studying to allow only as many coils of the string to circle the peg inside the box as to lock it conveniently firm. A very ingenious and neat contrivance has been invented by Mr George Withers, 51 St Martin's Lane, London, an engraving of which is given below.

The invention somewhat resembles a violoncello peg, but has a hollow in the broad head, lined with soft leather, which admits the whole of the head of the violin peg, which with the extra leverage thus lent can be easily moved, however tightly locked. Children and lady players with weak fingers will find this peg turner a great boon. The invention, which costs 2s., is made of ebony, with a strong ferule of brass round the head, and may be had of any musicseller, or direct from the inventor.

CHAPTER VI.

Violins, Old and New.

But man's life is too short to be all spent in adjusting a violin. TAKE OUT YOUR VIOLIN AND PLAY IT. A strange advice that may appear, but it is well worth being put in capitals. There are many who fondly imagine that they can acquire the requisite tone by other means than hard work and persistent practice. One of these is

The Adjuster.

The adjusting craze I can best describe by recalling an amiable and earnest amateur of my acquaintance. He had the fortune to possess a modern violin made by a Frenchman named Derazy. It was a pretty-looking instrument, of a bright orange colour, shading off into a kind of pink. The tone on the first and second strings was good, though small, hard, and clear; that of the third was poor and shallow; the fourth hard and wiry. The market value of the violin was about £3, 10s, but to its owner it was priceless—the best in the world He did not simply love that violin, he worshipped it A scratch on its clear surface, I am convinced, would have caused him more agony than a real scratch on his own skin; and had any mishap befallen the violin—had its ribs been staved in or the whole instrument been burned up bodily—I tremble for the consequences to the owner. Yet his playing seldom amounted to more than trifling with the violin. He was never quite satisfied with the tone, and would spend hours upon hours in adjusting and readjusting Six hours at a time was no uncommon stretch for him to closely engage in this task, and this went on, not for weeks, but always Bridges—he tried every kind; had whole boxes of them—soft, hard, broad, narrow, high, low, round and flat, thin, thick, seasoned and unseasoned—fitted in every way, and with all their merits and demerits written upon them in shorthand. Sound-posts—he had tried every kind, and every adjustable spot in the violin. Strings—he tried all kinds, and never had one on long enough to wear it through, or even flat on the face He had not time to play the strings through He wanted to get by mechanism at the tone which could only come by hard playing. One morning, when he told me of having sat for six hours on end and far into the night adjusting his violin, I could not help saying, "Ah, if you had but spent all the hours which you have for so many years devoted to adjusting your violin in good hard practice, what a grand player you would now have been! The tone which you are vainly seeking in the violin, you would long since have found in your own fingers. You want the violin to do the work instead of you." On another occasion, when I noticed that his strings were always round in the face as if little played on, he asked, what would be the advantage of having the string worn flat with the friction of the bow? and being told that the tone was fuller and better, as more surface was presented to the hair of the bow, he eagerly jumped at the idea by saying, "Then perhaps I had better rub down the face of the strings with sand-paper!" Mechanism—adjusting—anything but playing. Of course, I gave him up in despair. No violin is worthy so much attention and time in adjusting, and still less a new violin. Do not let the adjusting craze take possession of you. TAKE OUT YOUR VIOLIN AND PLAY IT. If after a reasonable expenditure of time and pains in adjusting the bridge, sound-post, and strings, you still cannot rest with your violin, get rid of it—sell it—exchange it—be done with it. As the editor once advised, in regard to a horse which took fits, "Take him at some time when he has not got a fit, and sell him to a stranger." Perfection in violins, as in wives, is a thing unknown, and what appears to you a fault may altogether escape the notice of another, or may appear an actual beauty. Speaking once to a dealer in strings, who got all sizes, thin, thick, and medium, I learned that he always sold out every box of them—those which did not suit one player, were eagerly bought by another. It is the same with violins. Have no compunction then about selling your violin. "Oh, I could not part with it," I fancy I hear some one say, as he clasps his beloved and faulty violin to his heart. Nonsense! You will have to part with it soon there is nothing more certain than that. Your violin will soon be in the hands of another, who will play upon it, and string it, and praise and abuse it, and coolly speak of it as "My violin." Death soon settles these absurd notions; you have only a loan of it at best for a little while. You may as well, therefore, make a virtue of a necessity, and part with it now, and get another more suited to your taste and requirements. Get as much happiness and as little irritation as possible out of the violin. That is its mission.

If you cannot part with your violin, and find, nevertheless, that it is weak or poor on certain strings, be content to let it remain so Take the tone as you find it, and rather have it weak and pure than thick and thready. Rather bear the ills you have than fly to others that you know not of. And let this fact console you—the ears of ordinary listeners are not trained to distinguish the niceties of tone as are those of a violin player, and a solo played upon a common German fiddle will often please as well as if it had been played upon a £700 *Strad.* It all depends upon the player. If he has full command of all the graces and arts of a good solo player, and is familiar with the instrument upon which he is playing, the audience will think only of the player and his power. The violin will be as good to them as the best Cremona ever made.

Frauds for the Experienced.

There is scarcely a violin in existence which has not faults of some kind, and I am not exaggerating when I say that there are at present hundreds of genuine old Italian violins selling at from £40 to £200 each, which are not, so far as the tone is concerned, worth £5 each. It is high time that these rusty old fossils sank to their real value, and that violin players above all ceased to sigh for their possession. It will be a boon to the world when they crumble into dust In selling these instruments it is not a question of tone at all. It is the "market value" that rules the price. In plainer words, "the rare old violin" is worth whatever you can get for it. Not one old violin in every fifty sold as genuine Cremonas, with written guarantees by so-called experts, is a Cremona. Many are old copies, good in themselves, and now nearly equal to the real instruments; many are by other Italian makers of inferior reputation, doctored, altered, and reticketed. Many of the violins of Stradivarius and Guarnerius, undoubtedly genuine, have spurious tickets, that is as certain as that the instruments are genuine. These violins speak for themselves without the tickets, which were too valuable to be allowed to remain in them, and have gone into instruments by makers less run upon. Therefore, when a ticket is undoubtedly genuine, be very suspicious of the genuineness of the violin Separating ticket and violin is creating two Cremonas out of one, turning £300 into £600 If the cheat can also separate breast and back, and apportion the ribs and neck among these, and mix up another old violin with them, he gets three Cremonas out of one. That has been done hundreds of times, and the frauds stare us in the face, and command high prices, gravely guaranteed by (highly paid) experts. Fashion rules in violins as in every other collecting craze, and the instruments of Antonius Stradivarius and Guiseppe Guarnerius being most run upon, are fabricated on every hand out of those of contemporary makers. A *Guarnerius*, therefore, at £80 would probably be dear, so far as tone is concerned, at £5. In the real instruments by these peerless makers the letters on the tickets are so coarsely executed, that it seems as if the stamp had been roughly engraved on wood, the spurious tickets are mostly printed from clean cut type on dingy coloured paper, though when a good paying fraud is being attempted the cheat will even engrave a block to exactly imitate the original. The genuine *Stainer* tickets seem to have been written, not printed; the spurious *Stainer* tickets are mostly printed from types. A guarantee from a London expert costs at least a guinea, and is often not worth a farthing. The tone is the only thing which cannot be imitated There is a maker at present in England who can imitate any instrument in appearance, but the tone of his *Lupots* and *Bergonzis* betrays the fraud to the practised ear—it is new, hard, and woody. But even these qualities may be softened somewhat by thinning down the wood of the breast immediately under the bridge. The tester looks only at the thickness shown at the *ff* holes, and never dreams of applying violin measuring callipers, even if such an instrument should be within his reach. The tone of the instrument thus doctored will be clearer and more responsive, but the instrument will not improve but deteriorate with time. About fifteen years ago a professional musician, bearing a name which used to be a spell to conjure by in regard to circuses, being located in Edinburgh, got a great number of tickets printed on paper of a pale brown colour, bearing the name of *Panorma*, and others of the makers less run upon, and stuck them into any violin he could get hold of cheaply, new or old, and had them sold for good prices in auction rooms. Some of James Hardie's violins were thus doctored, and curiously enough would now be worth more bearing the maker's name than they brought then with the fraudulent ticket. The famous case of Chanot and the "Carlo Bergonzi" violin must yet be fresh in the minds of readers.

The most reliable experts and dealers in this country, beyond all doubt, are Messrs. Wm. E Hill & Sons, 38 New Bond Street, London. An opinion on any violin may also be had, for a fee of five shillings, under the following conditions :—"As no personal interviews can be arranged, all instruments submitted must be addressed, carraige paid, to Mr. J. M. Fleming, 29 Frampton Park Road, Hackney, London, and be accompanied by a postal order for above sum; and all cases or boxes must have inside the sender's name and address on a separate label in a form suitable for attaching to, or pasting on, the outside of the package for the return journey. No package will be received if it is not carriage paid. A stamped addressed envelope to be sold for £20. When in Liverpool lately I called upon the head of a firm of dealers, who expressed a regret that I had not called the week before, as a remarkable bow had passed through their hands, an original *Tourte*, gold mounted, with an inscription to Lvoff, &c. My *Tourte* once more! He had sold it to a gentleman for £15, 15s I wonder if I shall hear of it again?" Since receiving the above account I see that Mr Fleming has noticed the case in his excellent articles on Violin-Making published in the *Bazaar*. I have often wondered what were the thoughts and feelings of Blank, the Vandal, as he laid his fine toothed saw across the wood of that splendid work of art to ruin it for ever. If he had known that he was to be so well spitted up to the hootings of the world for the outrage, I suspect the saw would have been thrown aside unused.

Another species of fraud on the experienced, is that practised by a certain maker, who though his own name stands high enough, does not hesitate to stamp his bows with the names of Dodd, Panorma, &c., partly obliterating the letters to give the appearance of wear, and hand these to his agents for sale. A bow worth £2, thus fetches £3, 10s. or £4, though the hand of the maker is stamped on the work much more truthfully than the name at the heel, and every inch of the stick is shouting out "I am new! fresh from the workshop! see, my varnish is scarcely dry!" The bow indeed may fetch a great deal more. All depends on the conscience of the dealer, and the simplicity of the buyer.

Genuine old Dodd bows may be picked up by the dozen, but in many cases the spring is almost gone. It is in the spring and balance of a bow that all the real value lies. Here again, however, it is not the state of preservation, but the name which rules the price, and whenever a dealer gets hold of an old Dodd bow he simply claps a modern nut on it, silver or gold mounted, and labels it from £3 to £10, according to conscience.

In regard to pattern, I am inclined to think that the preference of the old good bow makers for the septagon shape was based upon a sound scientific knowledge, and that a bow so shaped, all things being equal, will retain its spring and its straightness longer than one which is round. The stick must be straight as the stretched hair, and the curve downwards so strong and firm that for ordinary playing sufficient tightness of hair is got when the centre of the stick is only a quarter of an inch from the hair. If that distance be much exceeded before sufficient tightness of hair is got, the stick in that condition is of no great value. Any one possessing a bow which gives the requisite tightness with little screwing up, will always be careful that the above distance is not exceeded at any time through the ignorance of any one who may chance to use the bow The spring in the stick may thus never become impaired, and a good bow last through many lifetimes. Unless a fair proportion of the curve be left in the stick after screwing up, really fine playing is an impossibility. The stick should also be so firm that no quiver disturbs it when playing a sudden *forte* note. The bow must be suited in weight to the hand of the player and the instrument upon which he plays The tone of a very fine old instrument might in any but the hands of a great artist be killed by a very heavy bow, while a new violin might never yield its real tone until that was forced from it with a heavy bow. A bow should weigh not less than two ounces and never more than two ounces and three quarters. All the great violin artists use bows of about the latter weight, and through time the student will discover that a really powerful tone can never be produced with a light bow. If the bow be an old one, it will generally require a modern nut, with the slide fitted perfectly to the stick, so as to allow no movement to either side. The slightest yielding of the nut may warp the stick. The depth of the nut must also be suited to the size of the player's thumb, and wide enough to allow of a thin covering of leather at that part of the stick touched by thumb and fingers. Leather is always preferable to silver or gold thread, which being hard tires the thumb sooner, and is a constant source of irritation through giving way at awkward moments.

It is asserted that the spring of any bow may be restored, and I have known one instance of a valuable bow being thus put right, but how long the spring thus recovered will last I am unable to say. That would probably depend upon the wood of which the stick was made, and the treatment accorded to the restored spring by the player. The bow should never be screwed up tighter than I have indicated, and should be unscrewed till the hair touches the stick the moment the owner has done playing. Many are grossly negligent in this matter, and not only screw up the bow till it is nearly straight, but leave it thus when done playing. No spring in any bow that ever was made could outlast such treatment. I give here

Mr Fleming's recipe for the restoration of the spring of a bow, in which the element is heat:—"Take out the screw and coil up the hair towards the tip, so that you can hold it concealed in one hand, while you slowly pass the stick of the bow before a bright fire. Keep it thus, passing backwards and forwards until the stick becomes so flexible that you can bend it to any inclination or any reasonable curve. You can then rectify the cast and restore the bow to its original curve, if you know what that was. The heating of the stick will occupy from ten to twenty minutes or more, according to the intensity of the fire. You must be careful to pass it before the fire at such a distance as will save the varnish—2 in., 3 in., 4 in., 5 in., or 6 in. from the ribs, according to the heat. When you have rectified the cast, and given to the stick the proper curve, it will remain so. Carefully uncoil the hair and fix the nut in, leaving the hair quite loose, so as not to drag the stick. Then pass a piece of string under the arch of the nut and suspend the bow where nothing will touch it, and where it will cool equally over all the surface. You should not lay it down anywhere while hot nor suspend it against a wall. Half an hour or so will cool it. You must also be careful not to expose the hair to the fire, as it would shrivel it, and do not suspend the bow by the tip but by the nut. Glance your eye along the stick before suspending, in order to make sure that you have properly accomplished your task."

In the system practised by the clever artisan whose success I have just alluded to, dry heat, not steam, is also employed. His address is Mr Edward Brookfield, 1 Railway Street, Birkdale, Lancashire. He is a neat and trustworthy repairer of violins, and his charge for restoring the spring, or straightening a warped bow, is 2s. 6d. for a common one and 5s. for a valuable one, such as a *Dodd* or *Tourte*, the carriage both ways being paid by the sender. The spring can be restored without the least injury to the varnish, except in the case of common bows, when the varnish will not stand on account of its poor quality. In most of the music shops little cases of pasteboard or thin wood may be got in which a bow may be safely sent through the post.

Cleaning the Hair of the Bow.

The hair of the bow should never be so carelessly handled or kept as to need cleaning, but there are careless and young players who do get the hair dirty or greasy before it is worn too smooth for use, these may clean the hair thus—Screw up the bow pretty tight; wet the hair with cold water, rub on a good layer of common soap and then rub and scrape with the thumb nail till all the dirt and grease is loosened. Finally rinse off soap and dirt by turning a small stream of water on so as to run down the hair but not touch the stick. Slacken the hair well, immediately, as the drying tightens the hair, and will pull it out altogether if this be not attended to in time. Another plan: Take as much powdered borax as can be lifted on a sixpenny piece, put into a wine glass half full of luke warm water; apply this mixture to the hair of the bow with a piece of clean flannel; wipe dry with another clean cloth; and allow the bow to hang on a pin, free of the wall, for two or three hours, then apply rosin. If the bow get fair play, however, and be not used in dusty dancing rooms, and be kept in a case and not a bag, and the hair never touched with the fingers, washing will never be necessary. When the hair ceases to bite well, it will usually be time to remove it and insert a fresh hank. This should be done at least once every six months, though not a hair should be broken. Great soloists, and those who must have a quick response and a fine tone, renew the hair every six weeks or two months. A great deal depends upon the quality of the hair, however. The *Tourte* bows were originally fitted with exceptionally fine hair, selected hair by hair, by Tourte's daughter, who sometimes rejected hundreds before choosing one hair. Full directions for re-hairing a bow will be found at page 25 of *The Violin: How to Master it.*

CHAPTER VIII.

Tone—Forced and Developed.

There are two kinds of tone, which may be named the Forced and the Developed. We may occasionally see a violinist in some theatre orchestra laying his cheek on his violin, and tearing at the instrument with all his strength. His idea is that he is producing as much tone as two or three ordinary players. It is a delusion. The tone thus forced will not carry half-way across the pit. Its very strength kills it. The pressure of the bow must never be applied so coarsely or so strongly as to act as a damper, or to clog the vibration of the instrument; and the moment the note drawn forth ceases to be elastic, this killing of the tone surely follows. Any one unfortunate enough to get into this forced tone will never be a solo player, though he should play solos every day of his life. A fine tone is like a fine cathedral—it must be built up bit by bit. There are rules at the bottom, but the really fine player speedily gets above and beyond these. The first rule is to *play with the edge of the hair.* In exact proportion as the student plays with the stick of the bow inclined from him will be the fineness of the tone. If the inclination be marked and decided, the tone will be clear, elastic, and ringing; if there be but little inclination, or worse still, if he should play with the flat of the hair, the tone will be poor. How to keep the bow in that position and yet get the full benefit of the whole width of the hair, I have already shown in *The Violin: How to Master it*, p 46. The second rule is to play all rapid passages, which are not slurred, with the *upper half of the bow*, which is lighter and more elastic to the hand, and more pliant in quick crossings of the strings, than the lower end. The third rule is to play passages marked *piano* a little *further from the bridge*, and those marked *forte closer to the bridge*, at the same time diminishing or increasing the pressure of the first finger on the stick of the bow. But when by years of practice the student has mastered these rules, he goes beyond them. He may have a long note filling a whole bar of eight slow beats to play, with a *crescendo* or *diminuendo* on that note, in the performance of which it would be quite impossible to work the bow nearer to or further from the bridge. In that case he plays the whole note close to the bridge, making the difference in the tone solely with the pressure of the first finger on the stick of the bow. He does so for another reason than that now noticed. The hair of the bow can be better economised when kept close to the bridge—a most vital matter when a very long note has to be played. This acquirement comes to him in the light of a discovery, and by and by he unconsciously finds himself playing at the best part of the string to produce the tone required, and most often near the bridge. Again, he gets beyond a rule in regard to the use of the heel of the bow, and may begin a note marked *pianissimo* with the lower part, close to the thumb, and make a *crescendo* upon it as it nears the point. It is clearly against the rule, but rules are only for novices. They are the foundation only; the superstructure is left to the student himself to rear To understand practically what I have here laid down, it is only necessary to watch the playing of Herr Joachim or Madame Neruda. Get close to these incomparable artists, and if possible, at their right hand; and then observe the manner in which the tone is produced. The producer is not brutal strength, but refined art, built upon the basis which I have here tried to make clear. Technics first—the highest art after. First master the mechanism of bowing and fingering by the study of the ordinary rules, and then advance fearlessly into the region beyond. The difficulties of to-day are the trifles of to-morrow. Habit is second nature. And just as we who once spelled painfully through the short words of a First Primer, now read and master without an effort the most difficult words that it is possible to print in the English language, so that effort or attempt in violin-playing, which at one period seems daring itself, will at another be executed without a thought. Thus, to a novice at the violin, playing in the high positions, and shifting with perfect accuracy from the bottom to near the top of the finger-board, appears a marvellous performance; yet very shortly, as one set of positions after another is mastered, he finds that he can take certain of these shifts without a thought, and by and by them all, till at length he may play through half of the high positions in a piece without even remembering their name and number. He knows by instinct, as it would appear, but really by habit, exactly where the notes are to be found, and with what arrangement of the fingers they can best be commanded, and he takes that position. A pupil once stopped me in the middle of a solo, in which I had played a long passage pretty far up on the finger-board with the question, "What position is that?" "Position? really I don't know," was my answer, though by thinking for a moment and counting up I was able to inform him. Technics through time drop into oblivion.

A peculiar drawback from which all players upon all instruments suffer, is that they can never hear the tone they produce exactly as the audience hear it. The tone is never the same to the listener as it is to the player, though so far as the violin is concerned the difference is on the right side. This will be consolation to many a flustered solo player. The tone is generally better to the audience than it is to the solo violinist. His ear is close to sent along with the postal order" Outside of those there are many gentlemen amateurs, such as the Rev. Mr Hawies, quite as skilled, but whose services are only available through private friends and acquaintances; were it otherwise, the correspondence and labour thrown upon them would be quite beyond the power of any human being. The sum or application of all this is—become your own expert. Look at, and closely study the peculiarities of make and varnish and tone of every old violin upon which you can lay your hands. When done you will probably judge your violin more by the tone than by any other characteristic. With a genuine violin player the maker's name ought to weigh as nothing; the tone alone ought to be his criterion of value and worth, and in judging that it is necessary to consider its mellowness, its body, its purity, its ready response to the bow, and its carrying powers. The high-priced violin must be tested not only in the dealer's saloon, but at home, and in a large and heated hall, by both the intending buyer and an obliging friend, being diligently compared and contrasted against other violins, the powers of which are known to both I am taking it for granted that for solo purposes the player would always prefer a good old violin to the best new one that can be procured, though here and there new prophets have arisen who express a contrary opinion. There is in Germany a maker who asserts that he can make a violin or 'cello, with any desired quality of tone, equal to the best Cremona in existence. He also declares that he gets as high as £75 for a new violin, so constructed; but the statements of makers as to the prices they receive must be accepted with great reserve. If this last statement be correct, it only proves that there are violin buyers in the world who have a great deal more money than wisdom. No violin that ever was made is worth £75. As a rule violin makers are also poor judges of tone, and can seldom adjust their own instruments so as to get the best results, therefore they must be counted out altogether in an estimate of that quality. Counting the time, skill, and cost of material required to make a good violin, £20 is a high price for a new violin, and leaves a handsome margin of profit to the maker. Any amount above that sum paid for any violin is artificial, or acquired value, arising from the rarity of the instruments, the demand for their possession by collectors, or the mellowness imparted by their great age One need only take the best new violin that can be made into a large orchestra, to discover how lamentably small and poor his tone suddenly becomes, compared with that of other players beside him using violins mellowed with age, and how the violin must be "torn at" to get even that small amount of tone Any violin, however new, can be manipulated so as to sound well in a solo if the music performed be a slow piece. It is in playing rapid music, and more especially rapid chords, *arpeggios* or staccato runs, that the deficiencies of a new violin become glaringly apparent. It is hard work to get really fine music out of a new violin. Mr Heaps of Leeds, whose varnish I have noticed in the appendix of *The Violin: How to Master it*, professes to have discovered "a new principle" in the construction of violins, which renders the violin free of "wolf notes," and the tone exceptionally soft and fine, but he himself plays upon a very fine *Amati*, which was 90 years in the possession of one family. Mr Hardie, the Edinburgh violin maker, whom I have also noticed in that work, though making such excellent violins, played for many years upon a very fine old Italian violin. These facts are significant Mr Heaps exhibited a quartette of violins at the Great Exhibition 1851, which were universally admired, both for tone and workmanship. I have seen and tested one of his violins, made in 1866, from some exceptionally fine violin wood shown at the Great Exhibition of 1851, and bought by Mr Heaps at a high price. The violin feels light as a feather in the hand; the tone is rich, full, and equal, and the instrument a hundred and fifty years hence will probably be a grand solo violin I think it is not too much to say that better made new violins—except in the varnish, which will not compare with Dr Dickson's—are not in existence, as Mr Heaps, being a gentleman amateur and not making them to be sold, is not forced to work against time. Yet in a letter to me the maker says—"I do not think that the tone of my instruments is equal to that of old ones. Had I ever been vain enough to imagine such a thing, the *Amati* violin which I now possess would have taken the conceit out of me."

A great deal of fuss has been made lately, chiefly through advertisements, about the violins manufactured by a French maker named Collin-Mezin, which are sold at from £7 to £12, according to the conscience of the dealer Of course, they are advertised as made on "the new principle," that mysterious phrase which seems to convey a great deal, but really means nothing.

There is no new principle in violin-making, and there is no departure from the best models of the chief Cremona makers which does not mean inferiority. These Collin-Mezin violins are as clean cut and as like one another as biscuits stamped out with a mould. The varnish is of a dingy hue, and rather thin and watery-looking, giving the instruments a painted look. They are generally "roarers" in tone, and differ but slightly in quality, and to hear one tuned suddenly is enough to make any one with a sensitive ear almost jump off his chair. Tastes differ, but, for my own part, I should prefer to play upon a 50s. German fiddle, carefully picked out of a dozen or two, to using the best of these Collin-Mezin violins that I have seen. There is another maker, German, named Lowendall, whose violins seem to me preferable. The varnish is made to imitate that of the old makers, and sometimes with very questionable taste a portrait of one of the celebrated violin players is painted in oil colour in the middle of the back; but the tone is sometimes good, and certainly more mellow and soft than that of the Collin-Mezin instruments. They sell at £5 plain, and £5, 5s. with the oil portrait on the back.

If a new violin be wanted, however, there is no need to go to either Germany or France for one, much less to pay such a sum as £75. The ear of the young player is not very sensible to the finer qualities of tone; and for him almost any instrument, new or old, is good enough. When he has played for twenty years, he will probably be able not only to distinguish and appreciate the difference, and to draw out the good qualities of an old violin, but *to pay for one.*

There is a providence in all things.

CHAPTER VII.

Frauds for the Inexperienced.

I may now notice a class of frauds which can deceive only the most densely stupid and inexperienced, or worse, those who have a little of the cheat in their own nature.

In many of the leading papers small advertisements may be regularly seen, modelled after the following:—

VIOLIN FOR SALE.—Rich Solo Tone, appears to be very old, after and labelled "Antonius Stradivarius, faciebat Cremona, A.D. 1721." Splendid instrument, and in perfect preservation. Suit Young Lady or Professor. With good Bow, Case, and Self-Tutor, only 25s. Sent on approval

To these are generally appended a private address, with "Mrs Something" for the leading bait, as if the seller were a poor, ignorant, and unprotected widow, whom it would be easy to cheat, and who can know nothing of the enormous value of the article she is willing to sell so cheaply. Sometimes the advertiser takes a higher tone, and invests more money in his advertisement, after the following style:—

For immediate disposal, owing to death of my great-grandmother, a Grand Solo Violin. It is labelled after "Joseph Guarnerius [a long way], Fecit Cremona, anno 1725." Rare handsome antique-looking orchestral instrument; thorough preservation, exquisite rich powerful tone, suitable for professional, with snakewood bow, resin, instruction book, and magnificent brass-mounted lock-up case. Sacrifice whole lot for 15s. 6d., carriage paid anywhere; been valued at £4, 4s. Inspection invited, or write early and secure this genuine bargain.

It is of small moment what form the advertisement may take—the "bargain" is the same. The "lock-up case, resin, and instructor" might be thought, from the persistence with which they appear, to be enough to damn the whole thing, but no—the trade goes on as flourishingly as ever. The novice who sends his money to these dealers—if he get anything back at all—will probably receive in return a fiddle worth 3s. 6d., a case worth 4s., and a bow worth 1s. The fiddles are made by the gross, like penny pies, and the "rare antique" appearance seems to be done with white paint spurtered from the end of a well-filled brush, to take the place of the powdering of resin about the breast. One scarcely knows whether to pity the victim or pronounce him rightly served. It is as if one spider, wishing to trap a more simple spider, were to draw over him the skin of a tender and juicy-looking fly, and then place himself temptingly in sight of the other, as much as to say—"Come and eat me." The simple spider thinks he is about to do a clever thing, accepts the "sacrifice," and gets eaten up; but observe, they are both spiders. The man who expects to get such a list of articles as that offered in the last specimen for 15s. 6d. is nothing but a rogue in disguise, and can scarcely complain if he gets nothing for his money but some valuable experience. As for the other spider—the offerer of the bargain, who can at will draw over him the skin of a poor ignorant widow, or of an experienced professional musician—he must often be so hard pressed by his wrathful customers, that to condemn him here would be like trying to kick the life out of a dead donkey He used to deal in pianos, with wretched works and sticky notes, which were always to be sacrificed at a fourth of their cost, as the owner was, like all of us, tremendously in want of money. He was always a widow then. Violins have come to the front now, however, and he has, like a sensible tradesman, gone with the times and turned his attention to them. Lately one of him advertised a fine old violin and silver-mounted bow for 7s 6d A friend of mine, wishing to make some experiments with the sound-post, thought this a good chance of getting a cheap violin, and sent the money. The fiddle was a common sixpenny one painted red, with bow to match; and the letters of protest were, of course, never answered. A book might be filled with such examples, but there is a wonderful sameness about them all.

If you wish to buy a cheap violin, go to the best dealer in your neighbourhood, who will generally give full value, and exchange the instrument for a better when your purse has grown heavier or your taste more exacting. If you will buy through an advertisement, insist on seeing and testing the violin before sending the money, or date the post office order ten days later, so that you may have time to recall. The *Bazaar* newspaper is an excellent medium for such transactions, and if the system of deposit adopted by the managers of that paper be followed it is almost impossible that the buyer can be robbed. That paper is also the best for advertisements of old violins, and any one in want of such instruments can almost certainly be suited by watching the sale column for a time, and bargaining according to the safe system above mentioned The paper is published weekly, price 2d., at 170 Strand, London.

Frauds in Bows.

Though the gain is smaller, the ingenuity of the cheat is as often exercised in frauds in bows as in violins. There is the small fraud of stamping cheap bows with any name—Vuillaume, Dodd, &c.—likely to make them sell well, and which deceives only the inexperienced; but there is also the carefully planned and elaborate fraud for a higher stake, which is intended to deceive the expert. The same lady friend who was deceived in the small matter of the 7s. 6d. painted fiddle bought a bow from the widow of a clergyman for £5. The seller, in perfect innocence, declared her belief that the bow was a genuine *Tourte*, a maker occupying the same place among bow makers that Stradivarius occupies among violin makers—that is, king of all. The bow bore a gold plate, on which was engraved "A de Llvoff, le 9 Mars 1841," and was richly mounted in gold, including the point. The plate indicated that the bow had once belonged to Llvoff, the composer of the Russian National Anthem and director of the Emperor Nicholas's private band. The buyer happened to be in the shop of a well-known firm of London experts in Wardour Street, some time after, and showed them the bow, which, after a rigid inspection, only excited a peculiar smile. Pressed hard, they declared that the bow had been pieced under the leather, and that therefore the heel alone was Tourte's. Something induced her to suspect a well-known maker, whom she managed to see, and from his manner and answers, guessed that the piecing had been his work, and that his employer had been a Manchester dealer and expert whom I may name Mr Z. Following up the trail, the spirited owner took Manchester on her way home, and bearded the lion in his den. She thus describes the interview. "I introduced the bow, which as I removed it from its paper case, made me feel as though I were unsheathing the sword of justice. 'I think you know this bow, Mr Z.?' He flushed crimson, and then became pale, and stammered out, 'This is not a *Tourte* at all. I told the Rector's wife it was not worth £5.' His manner was most excited. I asked him if he was aware that it had been pieced. He said he was, but his discomfiture was so great that I had not the heart to proceed further. I had satisfied myself that *he*—not the dealers in London—had sold the bow to the late Rector, and that Z—— had first taken the bow to H—— for the purpose of having it tampered with; that H—— promptly refusing to lend himself to the fraud, Z—— had engaged the skill of Blank, and had thus converted one genuine *Tourte* into two false ones! I subsequently placed the bow in Chanot's hands for sale on commission, stating that only the lower end was Tourte's, belonged to Llvoff, &c. He sold it for £8 Shortly after I was told by an expert of a fine Tourte which he had been called upon to value, and which bore an inscription 'Llvoff,' and was mounted in gold. The impostor again! I was informed afterwards that it was the instrument—every little slip and scratchy note is exaggerated and magnified to him. All these are lost before they reach the audience. The soloist very often comes from the platform disgusted with himself and his performance, only to be astonished by others congratulating him upon the delight and pleasure they have received from his fine playing. The graduations of tone are also more palpable to the listener than the player—*piano* to him is *pianissimo* to them—*forte* to him is *fortissimo* to them—a swell on a note is more noticeable to the listener than the player—the quiverings of a *tremola* or beats of an open shake, more marked and rapid; and a note must be dreadfully false before it will excite comment. I am not aware if this peculiarity belongs to any other instrument, but I am certain of the fact so far as the violin is concerned. Let the student, therefore, studiously practise these arts of expression, certain that though the effort may appear feeble to him, it is not so to the listener, and further that any little slips caused by nervousness, the heat of the room or the sinking of the strings are mostly swallowed up before reaching the ears of the listener These are curious facts, which I have never before seen noticed (see also Preparing Strings for Solo Playing, page 33).

The Close Shake.

It is no exaggeration to say that the strongest desire and ambition of every amateur violin-player is to play the close shake well. "How *do* you do it? How on earth do you make that *tremola?*" said an amateur to me once in an orchestral society. "I have sweated over the attempt for two hours at a time, and yet I can't get at the secret." My prompt answer was, that there are studies in violin-playing much more worthy of having so much time devoted to them; but he quickly retorted that I had mastered the art, and could afford to say so—put him in the same position, and he might think so too. I placed his hand and fingers in the best position for a beginner (see *The Violin: How to Master it*, page 79), and in two minutes he was able to make a few distinct waves on one note. He had laid the foundation for making a close shake slow or rapid on any note or any position, and went back to his seat among the second violins as proud as Punch. Hundreds of violin players are in exactly the position of that young man—they have the ability, but not the knowledge, and that thought has induced me to devote a little space to the subject here, in addition to what I have already written The close shake is an imitation of that tremulous wave which often comes unbidden into the human voice during the performance of a strained note. Some singers, through ignorance or a pernicious training, introduce this wave so often that they eventually lose all control of the voice, and cannot sing a note without the detestable and irritating quiver rattling through it. Many good tenor and treble singers remain in the second or third class, who might easily advance into the first, but for this wretched and damning *tremola* A singer thus afflicted, or a harmonium with the *tremola* stop out, are the two things which any one with a sensitive ear wishes to be leagues away from. On the violin this *tremola* or close shake is not nearly so intolerable, yet even there it is often sadly overdone, and many violinists, like the singers above noted, seem to lose all control of their left hand, and cannot play a long note without the persistent trembling My earnest injunction, therefore, to the student before trying to throw a little light on the study, is, master the close shake, but do not let the close shake master you.

In some instruction books the student is told to "press the finger firmly on the string, and move the wrist back and forward," to make the waves of the close shake. That seems to me a very stupid direction. After studying the matter closely, I have come to the conclusion that the wrist has nothing to do with the movement resulting in the close shake, and that that movement comes from the fingers, or more strictly from the nerves of the fingers and hand. If the wrist moves it is not to cause the waves, but because the trembling motion of the hand reaches and affects the wrist. Far from pressing the finger firmly upon the note, and "sweating over the task," the more lightly the finger is held to the string the more readily will the variations in the tone be commanded. What is wanted to begin with is to give the nerves of the fingers and hand free play to affect the finger on the string, so as to cause that to alternately press the string close to the finger-board and rise from the finger-board, and this cannot be done with a deadly clench of the finger on the string That the wrist has nothing to do with the movement any one may prove for himself by slowly raising and depressing a finger without actually allowing it to quit the string. The result will be that variation from true to false intonation, which really forms the quivering beats of the close shake. All that is wanted is a power which shall make these beats rapid enough, and for that power we apply to the nerves of the fingers and hand. To allow these nerves free play the first condition is to get the hand as free as possible of contact with the violin. For this reason a beginner will generally find it easier to make a close shake with the hand advanced to the third position, as described at page 79 of *The Violin: How to Master it*, as the wrist there gets the support of the ribs of the violin, and so allows of the first finger being held entirely free of contact with the violin. The same expedient may be adopted for a time on the first position until the trembling motion is mastered, but the expedient must be only a temporary one, as there are good reasons why the wrist should never touch the violin while the first position is being played on. Besides, the close shake is often of great use in forcing tone suddenly on a note marked thus >, in the performance of which there would often be no time to bring the wrist up to touch the ribs. The best position for executing the close shake on the first position will usually be found to be that shown as the "Free Position" on page 15, more especially with a beginner, but hands and nerves vary so much that even that expedient is not always necessary. A player who has begun at the age of five or six has usually no difficulty in mastering the close shake, the nerves have been brought into play before they could be hampered by stiffened muscles, and in such cases it can be clearly demonstrated that the trembling motion proceeds almost entirely from the fingers. Those who have begun later may often have to begin the mastery of the close shake by exercising the muscles rather than the nerves, but in all cases much study and practice will be necessary before perfect command of this delightful grace is attained, with every finger and on every position. When the best position for perfect freedom is discovered, the following hints may be studied with benefit:—In making a close shake with any finger, allow the three disengaged fingers to quiver visibly in the air. Thus in making a shake with the fourth finger on G on the second string, Third Position, quiver with the first, second, and third fingers, and so on with any other finger or position. Some pupils, more especially when making the close shake on the First Position, find it easier at first to keep down the finger behind that which is being used for the shake, as the finger thus kept down then acts as a kind of fulcrum to the leverage, but that is only another of those temporary expedients which any player may find out and justifiably use till the art o.

making the nerves instead of the muscles do the work is acquired. In making a shake, either close or open, on the First Position, even if the forefinger be not absolutely free of contact with the neck of the violin as shown in the engraving, it must never press heavily on the neck, but must for the time allow the thumb, in the "Anticipating Position," to bear the brunt of the work of steadying and upholding the instrument. Absolute freedom is best; a very light touch next best. A heavy pressure renders a good shake impossible. For this reason the close shake is much more easy of execution on the violoncello, or with the violin held upside down, as the hand is not then hampered by the pressure of the first finger, but is absolutely free of contact except at the finger point and thumb. After learning to help the quivering with the disengaged fingers, the student must endeavour to gradually get rid of mascular power in making the trembling, and more and more induce the nerves to become the motor. Both muscles and nerves are soon fatigued by practice at the close shake. It is advisable, therefore, to arrange the study so that the notes to be quivered on come in at short intervals, so that the fingers and hand may recover from the unwonted exertion. If this be not studied, the hand—exactly as in the practice of the open shake—soon gets lamed, and absolute impotence for the time being is the result. In like manner, as in the practice of the open shake, the fingers must be turned well over the strings, and the thumb be kept well under the neck, as shown in the engravings illustrating the "Anticipating" and the "Free Positions," pages 15–16. The close shake may be practised at any time and at any odd moment, with a bit of wood or an office ruler held violin-wise to the fingers. Any exercises or studies, such as those already noticed in the chapter on "Flexible Fingering," which tend to split the muscles binding the fingers, and so make them more independent of each other, also aid the student in the acquirement of the close shake; indeed, the most rapid beats of the open shake are often materially aided by that nervous quivering of the hand which should be the sole motor in the production of the close shake, more particularly when the shake has been a powerful one, and is dying away into *pianissimo*, with the beats quickening rather than retarding Lastly, the close shake must be practised diligently until such perfect control of the beats is acquired that they may be made faint or loud, slow or rapid, at will. Many seem to imagine that their power with the close shake depends on the mood of the moment, as it really does with those who choose to risk that. Others are content with a very faint attempt at the quivering, which they put in spasmodically, and often at notes and passages in which it is clearly out of place. Others, as I have noticed, go to the opposite extreme, and quiver on every note, however short, till all control of the hand is lost, and like those benighted beings trained to sing in the "Italian style," they cannot produce a plain pure note. The remedies for these defects of style are Practice and Good Taste. The first is within the reach of all. The second with many is inborn, but where it is not it may be acquired by frequently watching and listening to our greatest players. It will then be discovered that these great artists frequently play an entire slow movement through, without introducing a single close shake; while others of a more impassioned nature are richly and profusely ornamented with this delightful grace. It is only those who aim at a cheap popularity who depend upon this grace as their chief attraction. The power to play smooth elastic notes in the faintest *piano* swelling to the loudest *forte,* together with the instantaneous, exact, and true stopping of the notes, is a field of true expression which is only too seldom explored, while every street player and burnt-corked Christy minstrel considers the close shake the best trick in his trade Either master the close shake, then, and keep it in subjection, or let it alone altogether. It is a great acquirement, but there are others infinitely greater.

CHAPTER IX.

Concluding Advice.

I have now tried to put as clearly and tersely as possible before the violin player the best, surest, and speediest means of obtaining great command of his instrument. When these hints are perfectly understood, there remains but one advice to be repeated—TAKE OUT YOUR VIOLIN AND PLAY IT.

The Earless Scraper.

In only one case must this advice be altogether withheld or even changed into—"Put it away, and never touch it again," and that is when the devoted and determined scraper has no ear for true intonation. Then indeed the violin, which is the most thrilling and delightful of musical instruments when well played, becomes the most intolerable and atrocious torturer in existence; and the more ambitious the attempts of the player, the further he wanders up on the finger-board, the more dreadful becomes the result. No musician, I am convinced, ever felt nearer committing a murder than when listening to the earless violin scraper. This determined student is usually profoundly unconscious of his false intonation, and will go on to the platform on every possible occasion, and perform a solo with the most unbounded confidence. He is never nervous. He is also never asked twice to play, and through time discovers that there is a great deal of malicious prejudice against his playing. The acme of the horrible usually comes when he plays the rapid *Coda* of his piece, all in chords, and then every one in the room but those who like him are earless wishes him ten thousand miles away, or nearly faints in the effort to look pleased. Sometimes the sense of relief is so great to the audience when the torture is over that they applaud loudly, when to their horror on comes the earless scraper, as nimbly as an acrobat, to play an *encore*. He goes through life under the impression that he is a violin player, and merely kept back by a little prejudice. No one cares to hint at his fatal defect unless prepared to make him an enemy for life. A great man once said, "I can supply you with arguments, but I cannot supply you with brains." You may supply the earless scraper with knowledge, but never with the power to play in tune, so, sadly be it said, the best advice to him is "Put away your violin, and never touch it again."

Practise Solidly.

If you have an hour to spare get the most practice possible out of that hour. Put a pile of studies on the music stand before you, without regard to order, except that the first be a severe one, and then play them straight through without pausing even to take the violin from your shoulder. Such practice gives great power of endurance and flexibility of fingering, and will often compress the advancement of two years into one. The student who pauses for five minutes between each study to trifle with the music, or snuff, or smoke, or think, never masters the violin He might as well attempt

E

to write an immortal poem while devouring a juicy orange. Never scramble through music. Play every note, however rapid the movement, clean and pure, whether the note be accented or unaccented. Most commonly the unaccented notes are quite buried and lost in a rapid movement. They should stand out as clear and distinct as their fellows, as the difference is more one of order and position than force of accent. Many players in their desire to force execution quite outrun clear articulation, pure intonation, strict time, true expression, and intelligent reading. There is a feverish haste instead of a delicious repose or masterly ease in all they do. The cause is scrambling.

Common Faults of Advanced Players.

A bad habit which is most easily acquired is that of gradually getting *sharp* when a long passage with much shifting occurs on one string. Those unfortunate enough to fall into this habit are often surprised, in playing a long monochord passage, to find when they sound an harmonic or an open string that the note appears intolerably flat. The explanation is that the notes preceding, though true in relation to each other, have been played more or less sharp in relation to the pitch of the string. The only remedy and preventative is to be particularly careful that the starting note is true in relation to the open string, and to occasionally test the position with an harmonic or an open string. Some play sharp only on the fourth string, but it is more common for the perverted fingering to run over all the strings. The player thus afflicted will play sharp in orchestra, and make himself intolerable to all near him, though his ear may otherwise be good enough.

Feeling for the Notes.

Another common and evil habit is that of sliding the fingers up to the true stopping of the note by way of giving more expression. This is one of the cheap tricks of street players, but the evil of the habit is only discovered when the player is among such a body of instruments that he *cannot hear* when his finger arrives at the true stopping. The fingers ought to descend instantly, like little hammers, well wielded, upon the exact spot of true intonation, and the habit of playing thus makes it a matter of indifference to the student whether he be playing a solo or in an orchestra a hundred strong. This feeling for the notes has no relation to the slide proper, which is one of the finest graces of solo playing.

Duet Playing.

Next to playing and practising alone must always be reckoned duet playing. The harmony producible by two violins is a little thin at best, and we are so accustomed to a full body of sound that a violin duet, pure and simple, is only too seldom heard in public, the usual remedy being to add to the duet the accompaniment of a pianoforte. The remedy is much worse than the disease. The playing of duets, nevertheless, is one of the greatest delights of the true violin player, and one productive of the happiest results. The persistent duet player is always a good reader and a steady man in orchestra, and always plays well in tune, the simple reason being that if he did not, no companion player would endure him twice. Of all the duets composed expressly for the violin by the great masters, none can approach those of Pleyel Spohr's Grand Duos are wonderful pieces of harmony, but on account of their difficulty they will never be popular. Pleyel did not take a very high place as a composer, but his violin duets for attractiveness, simplicity of harmony, and melodic beauty have never been equalled. They may be had in five sets, in the Litolff Collection, from Messrs Enoch & Sons, Holles Street, London, at 1s. 3d. and 1s. 6d. each set. This edition, besides being the cheapest, is the best published, as every twentieth bar is indicated in both parts by a letter, a great convenience to players who are apt to lose or run away from each other in a duet. Next to these, I should place Maza's Duets, which may be had from the same publishers, in six sets at the same prices They are pleasing and romantic in their character, full of melody and good harmony, and have as much soul in them as can be expected in French music. These duets may be taken in the following order according to the degree of advancement of the players :—

(1) Pleyel's 1st book, No 526—Maza's 1st book, No. 1123.
(2) Pleyel's 2nd book, No. 527—Maza's 2nd book, No. 1148.
(3) Pleyel's 3rd book, No. 528—Maza's 3rd book, No 1149.
(4) Pleyel's 4th book, No. 835—Maza's 6 Duos concertants, Nos. 1158-9.
(5) Pleyel's 5th book, No. 836—Maza's 6 Duos brillants, Nos. 1160-1

There is really no comparison between the two composers, and the above arrangement refers to the degree of difficulty alone The first of these are very suitable for young players. About the poorest duets ever written for the violin are those of Viotti, which are merely dry and mechanical exercises wedded into duets by a knowledge of harmony Viotti appears to have been entirely destitute of the melodic faculty; his violin duets are therefore "wooden" in the extreme, though good enough for imparting a certain dexterity of fingering and independence in playing. Three books of these duets, edited by Carrodus, may be had from F. Pitman, Paternoster Row, London, at 6d. each It is as much as they are worth An excellent book of 20 operatic duets is published at 1s. 6d. by Messrs Boosey & Co., Regent Street, London. They are not difficult, and some of them make excellent pieces for performance in public. The duets of Rode, Romberg, Mayseder, Spohr, and Campagnoli may follow these, each of these composers having special peculiarities, the study of which give great breadth of style and power to the duet player. Good violin duets are usually so arranged as to divide melody and accompaniment pretty equally between the two players, nevertheless, it is a good practice to exchange parts occasionally, more especially where the chords are intricate or the parts difficult. Pieces may also be had arranged for three and four violins, a list of which will be found in the catalogue of the Litolff Collection. These make the harmony fuller, and perfect intonation easier, and are an excellent preparation for quartette playing proper. Quartettes for first and second violin, viola, and violoncello are the nearest approach to perfect music which is to be found on earth next to that of human voices. It is a grand triumph to the violin player, and great relief to his finely trained ear, when he can put aside the jingling pianoforte, and revel in full deep harmony and perfect intonation without an accompaniment which is good only for hiding a multitude of sins. The violin player ought to put before him the formation or joining of a quartette party as the acme of his ambition and the crowning joy of his life Violin duets may be had by the bushel bearing the names of all the great composers, but as a rule they are adaptions "cnopped up" for the occasion by musicseller's hacks. They are a fraud on the buyer, and a libel on the composers whose names are appended to them, and usually about as effective as *The Messiah* arranged as a duet for two flutes. Let the violin player beware of these, for as a rule they are not, and never were meant to be, violin duets.

Orchestral Playing.

After duet playing as a means of advancement comes orchestral playing, for which duet playing is the best preparation. The player should get into an Orchestral Society as soon as he can be tolerated in one, and if there be none in his neighbourhood, let him try to form one, however poor. It will prove a sure road to advancement and musical culture, besides being a means of conferring innocent pleasure, and therefore a blessing, on others.

Solo Playing.

From orchestral playing to solo playing is an easy and natural step. In *The Violin: How to Master it* (page 88), I have given a list of easy and effective solos, and to these I may add a few more, of a somewhat better class of music, which will be found equally useful as studies and effective as solos. The prices include a separate pianoforte part, and the list is arranged in the order of difficulty.

"La Colombe," Entr'act, by Ch. Gounod, price 2s. (London: Metzler & Co., 37 Great Marlborough Street).

"Un Rien," by Prosper Sainton, price 2s. (London: Chappell & Co., 50 New Bond Street).

"Romance in F," by Charles Fowler, price 2s (London. Weekes & Co, Regent Street)

"Meditation," by Ch. Gounod, price 2s. 3d. (London: Schott & Co, 159 Regent Street).

Rode's "Air in G," price 1s. 3d. (London: Cocks & Co., New Burlington Street).

"Il Trovatore," Fantasia, by J. B. Singelée (London: Schott & Co., 159 Regent Street)

"Gavotte Stephanie," by A. Czibulka, price 2s. (London: Metzler & Co.).

Raff's "Cavatina," price 1s. 6d. (London: Schott & Co).

"Two Romances," by Beethoven, price 9d., Edition André (London: Augener & Co., Fouberts Place).

"Aria," for the Fourth String, from Suite, by J. S. Bach, price 1s. (London: Neumeyer & Co, Hart Street).

"Elegia," by Luigi Risegari, price 2s (London: Hutchins & Romer, Regent Street).

"Légende," by Wieniawski (London : Augener & Co).

"Adagio," by Louis Spohr, composed in Gotha, 1809, price 2s. 3d. (London · Schott & Co).

Ernst's "Elegie," price 1s. 1d., Edition Peter's (Augener & Co.).

Nocturne (Chopin's), by Aug. Wilhelmj, price 1s. 6d. (London : Stanley, Lucas, and Weber).

Mendelssohn's Concerto, price 1s. 1d , Edition Peter's (London. Augener & Co.). The *Andante* makes a delightful solo for many who cannot master the whole work.

"Lucrezia Borgia," Fantasia, by Prosper Sainton, price 4s. (London · Schott & Co.).

Others may be discovered and picked up from time to time as the player progresses. In selecting such pieces it is well to note narrowly the difference between a duet for violin and pianoforte and a solo accompanied by the pianoforte. A duet for violin and pianoforte is a perfect burlesque upon music, no matter how great the exponents. The attention is continually distracted between the two instruments; the pianoforte makes a bad foil to the violin, and the violin accompanying the pianoforte seems utterly degraded. The pianoforte is good as a solo instrument, and so is the violin, but they do not assimilate well in a duet. As an accompaniment to the violin the pianoforte does well, though it will not compare with the harp; but to give it snatches of the melody here and there, as in a duet, and make the violin accompany its tinkling notes, is like setting the cart to draw the horse. For the same reason, to elevate the pianoforte into a concerto instrument, seems to me like putting a crown on a court fool. When a violin concerto is performed, you think of the solo violin alone, never of the orchestra, so distinct is the individuality of the instrument; when a concerto is given by the pianoforte, you think more of the orchestra than of the pianoforte, and the solo passages come in as an interpolation which is endured rather than enjoyed. As a solo instrument, the pianoforte never really shines except in giving music of the brilliant "fireworks" school, as demonstrated by Rubinstein and Liszt. These masters knew all that the instrument could do, and never asked it to do more—second-class music from a second-class instrument. Whenever the highest music is attempted, the cheat is discovered and the poverty of the instrument revealed, but then, curiously enough, the cry is against the performer—"How cold he is! how soulless!" Alas! it is neither the performer nor the music that is soulless—it is the miserable impostor of an instrument, the pianoforte. On these points, however, so "touchy" are pianoforte players, every one must be a light unto himself. I give my impression frankly, but wish to force it upon no one. During the present century the pianoforte has received from both composers and performers an amount of attention and worship so far beyond its merits, that anything—even a little devotion to the bass drum—would be a welcome change. The reaction against that craze has now more than begun, and before fifty years have gone the pianoforte will be assigned its true place as an economical and handy imitation of the harp, and a tolerable and cheap substitute for a small orchestra. Anything beyond that is but the fashion of the day, and must perish. True art is not founded upon fashion, but is eternal, and soon or late shakes off all that is false and unreal.

In conclusion, I can only repeat to the violin player what I have already addressed to the child student in the *Young Violinist's Tutor*.

Dear Fellow Student,—You have now laid a firm foundation for the mastery of the most perfect and pleasing of all instruments, and taken to your heart one of the purest and gentlest sweeteners of life—the matchless Violin! From this stage your upward progress is sure, but its rapidity will always be in exact proportion to the enthusiasm and love which you throw into the work. Nothing that is great was ever accomplished without toil, but here at every advance new beauties and delights will unfold themselves to cheer you on your way. Determine to *master* the instrument—to gain such a complete command of its powers, as to be able to pour through the quivering strings and wood every thought and emotion which you are capable of conceiving or expressing in music. Then will come to you the glorious consciousness of having conquered, the proud knowledge of power. You will revel in that—glory in it—and be happy. In the drawing-room, in the orchestra, or on the platform you will be able to thrill out on hundreds the inmost throbbings of your own heart, and so far will have attained all that ambition or ardent love can sigh for. But take this thought with you from one who has trodden life both in sunshine and shadow, with this tender companion ever by his side In the violin you have gained the best companion and truest friend that earth can bestow. And as a human friend, when communing and sympathising with us alone, always seems a superior being to the same person when we meet him in the world; so your violin, in your study, in solitude and retirement, will rise to grander proportions than elsewhere. It will raise you above the earth, it will sob and sigh with you in sorrow, rejoice with you in gladness, console you in bereavement, cheer you in trouble, and gently lift from your heart that calumny which mean humanity ever heaps upon the truly great and pure. It will become to you a mysterious kindred spirit, part of your inmost life and being. Such a friend is worthy the most ardent devotion. You will give it that devotion now, for the study, once fairly entered upon, is as fascinating as it is pure and elevating; and the more you develop the powers of this friend and companion, the more you will love it, and the more closely will it entwine itself into all your sympathies and desires. You have to face hard study, daily practice, and constant attention to the styles and advice of the very best of players before you can gain that power, delicacy, and infinite variety of expression which have crowned the violin king of all instruments. It is impossible that all can be great violin artistes. Water can never rise higher than its source. But each young student should work as if it were possible for him to be one of the greatest, as all experience proves that the most eminent among men have often had least idea in youth of their own powers and their mission on earth. Happy, happy golden youth! when one hour's study is worth hundreds in after life. Dear young student! that time is yours now! It comes but once. Make the most of it, and you will bless your unknown adviser long after the poor hand and brain which now shape these thoughts are at rest.

APPENDIX.

Bach's Sonatas for Violin alone.

EVERY violin student who wishes to acquire the power to play the most intricate chords, and finger deftly the most startling changes and catchy phrases, ought to get Bach's six sonatas for violin alone, Peters' Edition, No 228, price 1s 8d Many musicians think Bach's music hard, mechanical, and antiquated, but such a criticism certainly does not apply to these sonatas, which are full of brightness and joy. They were composed indeed at the happiest and serenest period of Bach's life, and are a fit record of his feelings. The celebrated Ciaconna is included in this volume, and the whole work is one for a life time. Many attempts have been made to set an accompaniment to these matchless inspirations, but in every case the attempt has been in the worst taste —an excrescence instead of an improvement. The sonatas are comp'ete as Bach made them, and the greatest kindness any one can show them is to keep and play them so. The rapid movements must at first be taken at quite a moderate speed, great care being taken to finger and bow them exactly as they are marked, as this work, like most continental music, has been edited with great care and exactitude In no other work is the surprising delight of a fugue upon a single violin to be found; and whether the music be played for itself or not, there can be no doubt whatever as to its effect upon the player, and half-an-hour's daily practice at some of these movements cannot fail to broaden and deepen the student's power and style.

Women as Instrumentalists.

A great American musician recently expressed the opinion that women make quite as good instrumentalists as men. At first sight there seems nothing in the statement which any reasonable being should dispute But a little examination will show that the opinion is not supported by facts. One might indeed as well say, "Women make as good men as men." Women may indeed produce as good music as men, but when the production of that music depends on muscular strength, as in performing upon the violin or the pianoforte, the efforts of women must be lacking in *power of tone* as compared with those of men Even Madame Néruda, though a big muscular woman, with all her power and skill, has not the tone of Herr Joachim or Mr. Carrodus;

and, in like manner, when a woman wishes to produce on the pianoforte that power of tone which Rubinstein and Hallè get with the muscles of the fingers, she has to use the weight of the hand—in a word, has to *thump*. To any one who has studied physiology the reason is plain enough—the muscles are not equal in the two sexes, and, therefore, though the conception may be in the brain of a woman, the hands cannot reproduce it, and so convey the conception to the listener.

When listening to a solo on the violin played by a woman, one of two criticisms is generally expressed, no matter how great the executive ability of the player: first, "How sweet the music is, but how thin her tone;" or, second, "Her execution is good, but how harshly she plays" In the first, the player is probably content to produce good music, as far as her muscular strength allows her; in the second, determined to get fulness of tone, she sacrifices the music, forces the tone beyond her muscular power, and gets only harsh noise. She cannot, as with the pianoforte, thump, but she can press and screech and bite out the notes, which is only another way of saying that she can force.

Is there no remedy for this? I am not sure that there is none. I do not suppose that women, collectively, will ever be equal to men in muscular power; but I do believe most religiously that their muscular power could be developed—more particularly the muscular power of the fingers, hands, and arms. They can row, swim, drive, or ride; they can swing from the trapeze or the horizontal bar, they can golf (the legitimate long game, not the silly abortion played with a putter); they can play cricket and tennis; they can hammer nails, do cabinet work, wood carving, or brass retioussèe work, they can sweep floors, brush carpets, hoe weeds, and dig garden plots. Such work and exercise continued from childhood to womanhood must produce a good result, and give the power to produce more muscular music—in a word, give more power. Even a man who has not a muscular hand will not produce the full tone of one who has, unless he has developed the muscles by some such means as those I have indicated I once knew a man, a light little follow, with fingers almost as thin as threads, who could execute almost anything upon the violin, but his tone was as thin as any woman's Another I knew who had been a joiner in his youth, and his tone was as full, round, and rich as if the violin had been a violoncello. The secret of the whole is in one word—muscle However, here it may be noted that there is no absolute gain in physics—where we gain in one direction we lose in another, and *vice versâ*

Intricacies of fingering generally present fewer difficulties to a woman than a man, as her fingers are thinner and less stiffened in the muscles than those of the ordinary man, but this very physical peculiarity tells against her in playing fifths and masses of chords in which one finger has to command two strings The finger points are too narrow.

A woman has a delicacy of touch and refinement of instincts which give her a tone altogether different from that of a man, and though that tone is weaker, it is often sweeter and purer Develop the muscles, and the tone broadens and deepens, but this subtle characteristic to some extent disappears. There is, therefore, consolation to the woman of weak muscles. Here let me give one word of warning. Forcing the muscles is often more disastrous than forcing the tone The development must be steady, not sudden A friend of mine, a violin player, would draw himself up to the chin by one hand, and he burst the muscle of the wrist and crippled it for life; another, a pianoforte player, would strengthen the muscles of his little fingers by pulling on his boots with them, and he lamed one of them, possibly for life. We are born with a certain power of muscle, varying both in men and women, and a certain power of development, and beyond that none of us can go. To compare the sexes for the sake of disparaging one is foolish. They were never meant to be compared. They are different, and always must remain different; both admirable, both illimitable in power in their different spheres. But in both there is here and there a weak joint in the armour; and I have here indicated where one may be found, and strengthened not only for the battle of life, but for one of the sweetest and most entrancing arts which God has shed upon this beautiful world.

Arpeggio Staccato Playing: How to Master it.

I have been frequently asked by correspondents to explain how that delicate and fairy-like staccato springing of the bow used in arpeggio

playing is executed. I thought that I had already explained this easiest of all tricks of bowing by giving an example on page 101 of *The Violin. How to Master it* (price 1s ; Edinburgh. Köhler & Son, North Bridge), but, as some of my correspondents may not have seen that work, I here give a fuller example. To produce the effect there must be no attempt to separate the notes in the slur, the bow will do that itself The trick indeed is so ridiculously simple that few writers have thought necessary to explain the method. The first bar of the example is marked with ordinary slurs. These are to be played with the upper third part of the bow alone, keeping the wrist of right arm rather stiff, and having the hair of the bow a little tight; almost before the first bar has been finished the bow will of its own accord have begun to stutter on the string, and will produce, without an effort on the part of the player, the delicate separation of notes desired. The same effect can be produced upon three strings, or even upon two. In many classical works introducing this arpeggio staccato (such as Mendelssohn's Concerto, Bach's Ciaconna, &c.) the lowest note is strongly accented, though still with the upper third part, and thus forms an effective bass to the melody, or the accented note may be the melody, though underneath, and the remainder of the chord the accompaniment to that melody. In the example below I have chosen those chords which are easiest to finger in tune and most ready to produce the effect. The fingering of the chords in staccato arpeggios must be finically true or the result will be atrocious even to the most dull-eared listener. A sure method of forcing the bow to begin to pick out the notes in this delicate staccato, and to keep it doing so, is to cause the lower part of the right arm, near the wrist, to strike the groin at every down bow, keeping the whole of the muscles of the right arm stiff and taut.

THE YOUNG VIOLINIST'S TUTOR

AND

DUET BOOK.

BY THE AUTHOR OF "THE VIOLIN: HOW TO MASTER IT," &c.

OPINIONS OF THE PRESS.

"'The Young Violinist's Tutor' should be placed in the hands of all beginners, on account of the pleasing and attractive manner in which it is arranged. The Introduction gives some very useful hints on the study of this instrument, so charming when well played."—*Graphic*

"The author has evidently devoted a large portion of his time to closely observing the difficulties which children have to encounter in entering upon this study, and to judge by this work the time has not been spent in vain. This rational method of instruction will be found to be one of the best that has hitherto been made public, and we heartily recommend it to teachers and parents."—*Saturday Review*

"The aim of the author has been to make easier the work both of beginners and of the teacher. As most of the instruction books take for granted a certain amount of knowledge on the part of the pupil, there is ample room for a work which, like this, begins at the beginning The author is a violinist of experience, and the book furnishes abundant evidence of his thorough knowledge of his subject"—*Scotsman*

"We can heartily commend it as an efficient and trustworthy guide for young or old, who intend learning to play the violin. The collection of airs is most attractive, and they are all pleasantly harmonised as duets The author has put clear-headed practical instruction in every page. It will decidedly give a great impetus to violin playing"—*People's Friend.*

"This book is thoroughly practical All the tunes are well arranged as duets, so that the master need not follow the vicious plan of covering up his pupil's faults by superior playing, for he has the means at hand in a simple accompaniment for giving needful help in mastering the difficulties of time and tune"—*Norwich Mercury*

"As a beginner's method it could not be easier. The difficulties are reduced to a minimum by an exceedingly gradual and highly pleasurable course of study, and by the plainest possible verbal instruction. The author is clearly an enthusiast and a most capable instructor; and the course of study is almost entirely through familiar airs set as duets, selected with remarkable aptitude to ensure safe and smooth progress."—*Dundee Advertiser.*

"To learn to play the violin while young is universally admitted to be the only road to marked ability with that wonderful instrument; but where is the violin tutor which any child could look at without its brain beginning to reel? The author of 'The Violin: How to Master it,' who may fairly take credit for much of the impetus given to violin playing within the past few years, answers this question by producing a tutor which, with what we take to be a touch of sly humour, he says is 'arranged on an entirely new principle, in a pleasing and attractive manner, for the use of beginners' Certain success awaits 'The Young Violinist's Tutor.'"—*People's Journal*

"Thoroughly practical, and has our warm commendation."—*The Queen.*

EDINBURGH: E. KOHLER & SON, NORTH BRIDGE.

10th Edition, Now Ready, Pictorial Boards, 2s. 6d., Cloth Gilt, 3s. 6d.

TRACED AND TRACKED;

OR,

MEMOIRS OF A CITY DETECTIVE.

By JAMES M'GOVAN,

Author of "Brought to Bay," "Hunted Down," and "Strange Clues."

OPINIONS OF THE PRESS.

"Mr M'Govan continues to work with success the vein with which he has already done so well. It is a book which it is unnecessary to criticise When we say that it is eminently readable, written with good sense and good taste, and deals with difficult subjects with much tact, we have not gone beyond the truth nor done more than justice to a very praiseworthy volume."—*Spectator.*

"They are among the best specimens of the class of literature to which they belong. Mr M'Govan is a genuine artist in the detective line, and puts into his stories a touch of real human nature."—*Scotsman*

"In 'Traced and Tracked' are to be found some of the detective's most interesting narratives. There are no detective stories which surpass those of Mr M'Govan in real interest and genuine ability. They are fascinating to a high degree, and so well told that they well repay more than one perusal"—*Rotherham Advertiser*

"M'Govan does not keep strictly to crime, but gives occasional digressions into sentiment. For the rest he writes without affectation, and keeps his piety within bounds."—*Saturday Review.*

"'The very Dickens of detectives,' as he has been well called, his narratives at once fix the reader's attention, excite his sympathy, and satisfy his judgment. One admirable feature is his feeling for those who suffer for no fault of their own A proof of the popularity of M'Govan's tales is to be found in the fact that they are being widely translated into Continental languages"—*Sheffield Telegraph.*

"The ease with which Mr M'Govan retains his hold on the imagination and the sympathy of his readers, is hardly less wonderful than the skill with which he seldom fails to unravel a mystery."—*Norwich Mercury.*

"We know of no other detective who could clothe his memoirs in language so simple and effective. There is more here than intense realism. There is a vein of humour, and an occasional gleam of pathos which we may look for in vain in volumes of higher pretensions."—*Aberdeen Journal.*

"It is in tapping these sealed fountains of true humanity, and setting free the pathos and goodness that have been hid, that the secret of M'Govan's success lies. Many of the tales are touchingly beautiful, and appeal direct to the heart. There are also gleams of humour here and there, and there is fascinating interest in every page."—*Dundee Advertiser.*

"They are masterpieces—always life-like—and the story kept boiling from the first word to the last"—*Courant.*

"M'Govan discovers an amazing insight into the ways, the thoughts, the feelings and the frailties of poor fallen humanity, and wields the ready pen of a perfect master of narrative composition"—*People's Journal.*

"For downright ability, sustained interest, and healthfulness of tone, we know of no stories superior to these experiences of M'Govan, and the present volume is every whit equal to its predecessors."—*Inverness Courier.*

EDINBURGH AND GLASGOW: JOHN MENZIES & CO.

LONDON: SIMPKIN, MARSHALL, & CO.

Lightning Source UK Ltd.
Milton Keynes UK
UKHW021849231222
414411UK00005B/159

9 780342 707683